WHO AM I?

ADEKEMI ADEBIYI

SYNCTERFACE™

Syncterface Media

London, UK

www.syncterfacemedia.com

WHO AM I?

ISBN: 978-0-9565043-2-6

Published in the United Kingdom by

SYNCTERFACE™

Syncterface Media
London
www.syncterfacemedia.com
info@syncterfacemedia.com

Cover Design: SyncterfaceMedia

This book is printed on acid-free paper

"There is no way you can see the glory of God without seeing Jesus and there is no way you can see Jesus without seeing His Word."

Dedication

To God Almighty, for the inspiration to write this book and making this dream a reality. All glory and honour to Him.

&

To everyone seeking to discover and understand WHO THEY ARE and aiming to live a full life. You will certainly be and do all that God Almighty had designed for your life.

Acknowledgement

I appreciate the efforts of the people who have contributed to this book.

To my Family:

I could not think of a greater family than mine and I am truly honoured and blessed by everyone of you.

To my precious mother *Affiong*, for loving me unconditionally and showing me the path of truth.

To my sister *Adeola*, may all your beautiful dreams come true.

To *Uncle Manny & Aunty Dupe*, for your selfless support and encouragement you are invaluable.

To my *Tiffany and Tianna*, may your true potentials be maximized in your generation.

To *Aunty Muriel*, for your love and support.

To my friends and colleagues at Jesus House London:

To *Luke Joseph*, whose commitment to the work and vision to make this book a reality. For your time spent in typing this manuscript, I am forever grateful to you and will uplift you in my prayers.

To *Deborah Owhin, Edward Duke, Tsakani Mthimkulu, Gus Miller, Mr & Mrs Olusunmade Ejiwunmi, Ekaette Isokhari, Adekunbi Adubifa, Sarah Elliot, Bosun Shadare,* for your support and encouragement. I appreciate you all.

To *Mr & Mrs Olaoshun, Bitrus Bulama, Mr & Mrs Winston Ekpo, Mr & Mrs K Jordan, Aunty Jumoke*. Thank you for your support. God reward you abundantly.

I especially want to thank *Jennifer Enwezor & Sele L. Gyang,* for believing so much in me and encouraging me in the pursuit of this dream and proof reading the book time and again. I am truly blessed to have you as friends.

My deep appreciation goes to *Pastor Agu Irukwu, Pastor Shola Adeaga, Pastor Bajo Akisanya, Pastor Bukola David Olanrewaju, Pastor Obasa, Deacon Ayo Adedoyin,* for all your contributions, advice and spiritual inspirations you have left me with.

To *Mr Akin Akinyemi,* I am eternally grateful to you. You have inspired me to achieve greater heights.

Contents

Chapter 1

The Question

*D*efining who you are is always going to be an interesting conversation to have. Can you define yourself if you did not create yourself? When you look at a piece of art created by an artist, there are many permutations of interpretations that can be read, particularly when it is an abstract art. The same way, when asked to describe who you are, the descriptions given usually depend on the person giving the description. For example, your parents give one description which may be different from what your friends will give, much more the description your employer will give or the one your brothers or sisters will give.

Knowing that all these descriptions will depend on which side of you each of them had experienced can be a bit scary. Which description will be right? What if the side of me they saw was when I was experiencing a down time in my life? What if someone only knew of the experience of Jesus being crucified and never heard of the resurrection, what description of Jesus would they give? What if they only know about the resurrection and know nothing about his sufferings? Is there anything that I can look at to determine the complete picture? Is there a manual that describes who I am supposed to be?

Many individuals go through life seeking answers to questions like these. Is there a reason for my being? What does this life have in store for me? Some find their path in life while others do not, some wonder around seeking a better life while some do not even know what to expect. Sadly, many wrong things determine the quality of life we live; family, friends, and society. What the larger society dictates as the standard of living is what is accepted. Interestingly, if we take a closer look at what the larger society defines as life and how it should be lived, we would see that it is ever evolving, minds keep changing as to what should be the basic values of life. How much more the complex issues of identity?

The family unit used to be closely knit and was the bedrock of any society but that has evolved in the era of liberalization where accomplishments are more important than family values. Relationships have witnessed a major decline; parents are no longer important and are dispensable, moral values are fast becoming a thing of the past. The elderly are abandoned to their fate, animals now replace family, people are alienated from one another, you wonder then why there is so much chaos in this day and age. It has evolved into an "all of me" world and anything else can follow. Love has been redefined and people defined based on the circumstances in their life.

Crime rates are high, divorce rates are at its peak, the institution of marriage has been watered down into partnerships legal or otherwise. People are insensitive and intolerant towards one another, hatred in all forms shape and size is an open show, image is everything and substance is nothing. Religion has become a fashion statement or more so a social club. Different doctrines are springing up daily, different religious sectors are on the rise to fuel man's thirst for a higher power, to fill the void in his soul and connect to his Creator. Some allege there is no God, others say there is a God but He must be extremely wicked to sit up there and allow so much wickedness reign.

Well, I am here to tell you about an extremely good God, a constant by whom we can answer the complex questions of life. Choosing to follow this path of life is the best decision you would ever make in your entire life time. There is the beckoning of the Lord to turn to Him. Jesus died for the sins of the whole world so that we do not perish in eternity. He went through the worst to ensure that we have life in abundance. He was nailed on the cross and He shed His blood that we may be reconciled to our Maker and Father in heaven. All this He did because He loves us, not the type of love the world offers but love that endures and cannot be broken. If you do not know Jesus or have a relationship with Him, this would really be a good time for you to open your heart and accept Him and your life will never be the same again.

Starting a brand new life with God is just the beginning of it all; this book will help you discover who you are and how to walk with God. Be expectant as your Maker answers the hidden questions of your heart from the pages of this book.

Chapter Summary

When asked to describe who you are, the descriptions given usually depend on the person giving the description

He went through the worst to ensure that we have life in abundance.

Chapter 2

Who Am I - The Answer?

I believe there are two ways to attempt to provide an answer to the question *"Who Am I?"* We could use the general societal approach where we answer the question based on what we know about ourselves, our work achievements, our culture or our background. We define ourselves by external attributes, what we can see physically and by standards that society has set. The challenge with this approach is that the standards of society changes and more often than not, value and belief systems do not form part of that definition.

We could also choose to answer the question based on what we believe someone has said about us. In this case, we shift the definitions away from what society or experience has to say and tilt towards what this *"someone"* has to say. For example, have you considered how often you have heard parents say their children are shy? Or how often parents describe what their children are not? In a lot of cases, these children will define themselves based on what they have heard their parents and others say about them. So as the child grows up, they start to say things like *"I'm a very shy person"* and guess what? Unless an external influence alters this perception, these children tend to grow up being *"reserved"* people, needing the affirmation of others. So the real question is this? What if the parents spoke different words, what if they said things like *"He is an extremely confident child"* irrespective of the physical attributes being exhibited by the child, would the child grow up more confident?

It appears then that, generally, we have a need for two critical elements to be included in whatever answer we give to the question, **Who Am I?** The first is *the need to exercise belief* while the other is to *exercise this belief in the words spoken by someone.* You may ask the question, how can I believe in someone to define who I am? Well, think, maybe you already have. I remember a story once when this very question was being discussed and one of the people involved in the discussion disagreed visibly with this approach saying I cannot believe in anything that has not or cannot be scientifically proven. After going on a rant for quite a while, another person in the discussion then asked a question. *"How do you know your parents are your biological parents, have you done a DNA test to confirm their legitimacy as your parents?"* Dead silence filled the room as the penny dropped. All his life, he had called two people *"daddy" and "mummy"* based on the relationship he had with them and the things they did for him. He had believed in the words of *"daddy and mummy"* in defining his identity and inclusion in a family.

If this be the case, who is the *"someone"* whose words you would believe? Who is the *"someone"* whose words have defined the identity you have adopted? In the case of this young man we just talked about, what better option does he have to provide an answer to that question than to go to *"daddy and mummy"* for an answer? What if *"daddy and mummy"* themselves are not sure? I suggest you keep going up the chain until you get to the One who is at the beginning of it all, the One who has no beginning of days, who was before all and who created all. If I can get this One to answer the question, then maybe I can switch the words I have believed and become a member of another family and finally find an answer to my question. *Who Am I?*

I am sure that by now you realise that there is only one person that history reveals who fits the description given above. Many *"someone's"* have come but only one has so far withstood the test of time to fit our description.

> ¹³ *For when God made promise to Abraham, because he could swear by no greater, he sware by himself,*
> ¹⁴ *Saying, Surely blessing I will bless thee, and multiplying I will multiply thee.*
> ¹⁵ *And so, after he had patiently endured, he obtained the promise.*
> ¹⁶ *For men verily swear by the greater: and an oath for confirmation is to them an end of all strife.*
> ¹⁷ *Wherein God, willing more abundantly to shew unto the heirs of promise the immutability of his counsel, confirmed it by an oath:*
> ¹⁸ *That by two immutable things, in which it was impossible for God to lie, we might have a strong consolation, who have fled for refuge to lay hold upon the hope set before us:*
> ¹⁹ *Which hope we have as an anchor of the soul, both sure and stedfast, and which entereth into that within the veil;*
> ²⁰ *Whither the forerunner is for us entered, even Jesus, made an high priest for ever after the order of Melchisedec.*
> ¹ *For this Melchisedec, king of Salem, priest of the most high God, who met Abraham returning from the slaughter of the kings, and blessed him;*
> ² *To whom also Abraham gave a tenth part of all; first being by interpretation King of righteousness, and after that also King of Salem,*

which is, King of peace;
³ Without father, without mother, without descent, having neither beginning of days, nor end of life; but made like unto the Son of God; abideth a priest continually.

Hebrews 6:13-7:3

²⁰Where Jesus has entered in for us [in advance], a Forerunner having become a High Priest forever after the order (with the rank) of Melchizedek
¹FOR THIS Melchizedek, king of Salem [and] priest of the Most High God, met Abraham as he returned from the slaughter of the kings and blessed him,
²And Abraham gave to him a tenth portion of all [the spoil]. He is primarily, as his name when translated indicates, king of righteousness, and then he is also king of Salem, which means king of peace.
³Without [record of] father or mother or ancestral line, neither with beginning of days nor ending of life, but, resembling the Son of God, he continues to be a priest without interruption and without successor.

Hebrews 6:20-7:3 (AMP)

From the above scripture, it is only right to answer the question from God's perspective. Whether you believe in Him at this stage or not, give Him a chance to make His case. Given His record of existence, He may be right. So an appropriate question to ask at this stage is *"**Who Does God Say I Am?**"*

Chapter Summary

How can I believe in someone to define who I am?

Who is the "someone" whose words have defined the identity you have adopted?

Maybe I can switch the words I have believed and become a member of another family

Chapter 3

Who Does God Say I Am?

*E*verything God says you are starts from a foundation. Who God says you are is a position you grow into. One of the first things God says about you is that you have the opportunity to become a son in His family. I call this an opportunity because even though God has made the provision available for you to become a son, you still need to follow the process of accepting the offer.

> *¹² But as many as received him, to them gave He power to become the sons of God, even to them that believe on his name:*
>
> *John 1:12*

For you to be able to claim the rights of sonship in the family of God, remember you will need to exercise belief in what God has said about you. So if God says you are a son, what do you have to exercise belief in to make this sonship a reality? Apostle Paul gave us the answer to this in his epistle to the church in Rome.

> *⁸ But what saith it? The word is nigh thee, even in thy mouth, and in*

thy heart: that is, the word of faith, which we preach;
⁹ That if thou shalt confess with thy mouth the Lord Jesus, and shalt believe in thine heart that God hath raised him from the dead, thou shalt be saved.
¹⁰ For with the heart man believeth unto righteousness; and with the mouth confession is made unto salvation.

Romans 10:8-10

I have always wondered why this process involved just believing and speaking until I realised this is the only way this sonship can be made available to all without prejudice. One of the things you find about this foundational process of joining the family of God is that it is available to any man or woman. God Himself reconciled us to Himself. This means God does not discriminate against any man or woman that comes to Him.

¹⁷ Therefore if any man be in Christ, he is a new creature: old things are passed away; behold, all things are become new.
¹⁸ And all things are of God, who hath reconciled us to himself by Jesus Christ, and hath given to us the ministry of reconciliation;

2 Corinthians 5:17-18

This process of believing in our hearts and confessing with our mouths what we believe is equivalent to the process of being born into a natural family. There are only two ways of becoming a member of a family. You become a member of a family either by adoption or by birth. Being born into the family of God is membership by adoption. To all that receive Him, they experience being born by the word of God

¹⁸ Of his own will begat he us with the word of truth, that we should be a kind of firstfruits of his creatures.

James 1:18

Those born of God are His choice possession. They are the apple of His eyes. They are defined as a people who are co-heirs with Christ (*Romans 8:17*). You are a chosen generation, a royal priesthood, a holy nation that should show forth the praises of Him who has called you out of darkness into His marvellous light (*1 Peter 2:9*). *Matthew 5: 13-16* describes you as the light of the world and the salt of the earth. You are definitely not a mistake. Even if you do not know your biological parents or you were told you were a mistake you are no mistake to God. He knows your name and knows every detail about you. He knows the number of hair on your head and you are valuable to Him (*Luke 12:7*). He already predestined you before you were born for a reason (*Jeremiah 1:4*). He loves you for who you are.

> *²⁶ And God said, Let us make man in our image, after our likeness: and let them have dominion over the fish of the sea, and over the fowl of the air, and over the cattle, and over all the earth, and over every creeping thing that creepeth upon the earth.*
> *²⁷ So God created man in his own image, in the image of God created he him; male and female created he them.*
> *²⁸ And God blessed them, and God said unto them, Be fruitful, and multiply, and replenish the earth, and subdue it: and have dominion over the fish of the sea, and over the fowl of the air, and over every living thing that moveth upon the earth.*
>
> *Genesis 1:26-28*

You are created in the image and likeness of God. When He was done creating you, He looked at you and saw that you are were good and blessed you. You are fearfully and wonderfully made (*Psalms 139:14*). God has so much to say about who you are. God does not have any reason to prove Himself to you. With or without you, He is still God. God is not a man for Him to lie, neither is He human that He should change His mind.

> *¹⁹ God is not a man, so he does not lie. He is not human, so he does not change his mind. Has he ever spoken and failed to act? Has he*

ever promised and not carried it through?

Take your time to meditate on these scriptures to reset your mind to what God has said. You have established who God says you are from His Word so begin to think of yourself as one.

Our redemption cost the most expensive price you can imagine. It cost God, the life of His Son. All of the things God declared you to be is as a result of what Jesus did on the cross of Calvary. It is therefore important to have a good understanding of what really took place on the cross, in death, resurrection and ascension.

What is this salvation all about?

The Bible states clearly in *Romans 3:23* that all have sinned and fallen short of God's glory. Man's progenitor ADAM fell from grace and introduced sin and a knowledge of evil he did not know how to handle. This stumbling repeats itself every time we disobey the voice of God.

Salvation is God restoring the relationship He had with man before the fall of Adam. Through salvation, we are recreated in the image of God, we possess in us His divine disposition and become His representative here on earth. We are created as gods here on earth. Salvation is established on God nature, Love. God is love (*1 John 4:8*) and without this love, there will be no salvation. God vividly demonstrated His love by giving up His only Son Jesus to die for us. *John 3:16* says "*He so loved the world that He gave His only begotten Son that whosoever believes shall not perish but have eternal life*". He loves you and I so much that nothing was out of reach for Him to pay for our redemption, He paid a costly price (*1 Corinthians 7:23*) to redeem our souls. For there is no greater love than this, that a man will lay down his life for his friends (*John 15:13*), we are no longer servants and Jesus declared us friends, everything we are and have are based on the love of God.

Jesus was offered to be the sacrificial lamb of atonement to cleanse us from the guilt of our sinful nature. He redeemed us from the curse of the law (*Deuteronomy 27:26, Deuteronomy 28:15-68*). The bondage of eternal damnation is what He redeemed us from, so when Jesus was hung on the cross, He took away the curse and the consequences of the curse. God demonstrated His unfailing, unwavering love for us that while we were yet sinners Christ died for us. God did not wait until we did the right thing but made us right through His love. He taught us what love is all about, and not what the world has defined love to be, worldly love is based on unstable emotions and feelings, love that withers away and is destructible. Love that causes pain and anguish that cannot be relied upon. God's love is stable, purposeful and determined, love that remains and can be relied on when all else fails.

God takes everything that concerns us seriously. From a life of sin, bondage and condemnation, He transformed us into the kingdom of light and declared you a child of light. Through salvation, Jesus has made us bona fide citizens of the kingdom of heaven (*Philippians 3:20*).

Chapter Summary

Who God says you are is a position you grow into

Believing and speaking.....is the only way this sonship can be made available to all without prejudice

You become a member of a family either by adoption or by birth. Being born into the family of God is membership by adoption

Salvation is God restoring the relationship He had with man before the fall of Adam

Chapter 4

The Promise And My Inheritance

A person who is not in Christ is cut off from God and cannot appropriate the promises God has made available for His children. In fact, such a person is without God in this world but by becoming a believer, blessings that were once unavailable to you can now be yours. Salvation brings with it restoration, which is one of the many gifts of God through Christ Jesus. I urge you to get a good understanding of this chapter because it defines a lot of things for you as a believer in Christ.

The Promise To Abraham

Salvation can be viewed as the fulfilment of a promise God made to Abraham in *Genesis 12:1-3*.

> *¹ Now the LORD had said unto Abram, Get thee out of thy country, and from thy kindred, and from thy father's house, unto a land that I will shew thee:*
> *² And I will make of thee a great nation, and I will bless thee, and*

make thy name great; and thou shalt be a blessing:
³ And I will bless them that bless thee, and curse him that curseth thee: and in thee shall all families of the earth be blessed.

Genesis 12:1-3

Abraham, a gentile, who was at the time an idol worshipper, was called out to a high calling of service, to be separated from his people unto great works. In *verse 3,* the Lord in honouring Abraham's obedience, pronounced *"that in thee (Abraham) shall all the families of the earth be blessed".* This was the beginning of the promises of God to Abraham. In *Genesis 13:15-18,* the Lord makes further promises to Abraham regarding his unborn generations and what their inheritance would be in Him. He shows him the extent of the blessings that will come to him and generations after him by using imagery that Abraham could relate to.

¹⁵ For all the land which thou seest, to thee will I give it, and to thy seed for ever.
¹⁶ And I will make thy seed as the dust of the earth: so that if a man can number the dust of the earth, then shall thy seed also be numbered.
¹⁷ Arise, walk through the land in the length of it and in the breadth of it; for I will give it unto thee.
¹⁸ Then Abram removed his tent, and came and dwelt in the plain of Mamre, which is in Hebron, and built there an altar unto the LORD.

Genesis 13:15-18

In *Chapter 15:1,* God reveals Himself in a different light to Abraham, as his shield and exceeding great reward. At this time, Abraham was childless and was looking likely to be succeeded by his servant. However, though he was not sure how all of these things promised were going to take place, he spoke to the Lord about not having a heir or seed to inherit all the promises of God and the Lord promised Abraham that his servant would not be his heir but his wife Sarah would bare him a son who would be his heir and Abraham believed all that God promised him.

In Abraham's days, covenants were used to seal an agreement to make it unbreakable. He therefore, requested a surety from the Lord regarding all that He had spoken. This surety or covenant operated just like contracts in this present day but covenants carry much more weight than contracts primarily because the only way to exit a covenant is by death or one of the parties.

In *verse 8-21* of *Genesis 15*, we see the covenant God entered into with Abraham as a seal to the promises that He had made. The covenant made the promise sure. It was settled at this point and there was no going back. Abraham knew what to expect from God and God had His expectations of Abraham. God had spoken and His word could not return to Him without accomplishing what He had purposed.

According to the terms of the covenant, Abraham was God's responsibility and obedience was Abraham's obligation and so an everlasting partnership was formed. In *Genesis 17*, the Lord reiterates His covenant with Abraham but now the wording of the promise changes from what we have seen in the previous chapters. It changes from promise to covenant. He clearly mentions that His covenant is with Abraham and not just a promise.

> *⁴ As for me, behold, my covenant is with thee, and thou shalt be a father of many nations.*
>
> *Genesis 17:4*

He states the nature of the covenant in *verse 7* as an everlasting covenant. A covenant that extends to all of Abraham's seed as long as the earth remains.

> *⁷ And I will establish my covenant between me and thee and thy seed after thee in their generations for an everlasting covenant, to be a God unto thee, and to thy seed after thee.*
>
> *Genesis 17:7*

It is the Lord who made and established the promise and covenant. Abraham's part at this point in honouring the terms of the covenant was to ensure that all the male children and man servants in his entire house were to be circumcised. As long as these terms were adhered to, the Abrahamic covenant stood. This act of circumcision was to seal the promise.

The covenant is again declared an everlasting covenant in *verse 19*.

> ¹⁹ *And God said, Sarah thy wife shall bear thee a son indeed; and thou shalt call his name Isaac: and I will establish my covenant with him for an everlasting covenant, and with his seed after him.*
>
> Genesis 17:19

God did answer Abraham's request and a heir of the covenant, Isaac was born to Abraham at the age of one hundred. This happened when all hope of child bearing or reproduction had ceased for both Abraham and Sarah. The things of the kingdom of God are usually done to ensure that no man can take glory for them and to demonstrate God as being all powerful, a God that is not bound by the limitations known to man.

What was God doing through Abraham and this covenant? He was introducing to humanity, the concept of salvation through a *"seed"* or single source.

Looking at *Genesis 22:18*, the Lord declared to Abraham stating *"in thy seed shall all the nations of the earth be blessed because thou obeyed my voice"*. Prior to this time, in *Chapter 12:3 "in his seed shall all families of the earth be blessed"*. This *seed* referred to here is definitely not Isaac, for the whole earth is not blessed by Isaac but rather through him. It is Jesus who blesses the whole earth. The blessing came through Isaac.

> ¹⁷ *His name shall endure for ever: his name shall be continued as long as the sun: and men shall be blessed in him: all nations shall call him blessed.*
>
> *Psalm 72:17*

Jesus Christ is the one who came to save the whole world from sin and death. You can read the genealogy of Jesus in *Matthew 1* and *Luke 3:21-38*. The promise that the whole world would be saved by the seed of Abraham is seen in *John 3:16-17*. The fact that *the only begotten Son of God* is sent into the world to save the world and not condemn it, is the blessing referred to in *Genesis 21:2*. The blessing of salvation is for all the families of the earth, as long as you believe, you are saved. Salvation was rooted in these promises but not many understood it then.

Apostle Paul in *Galatians 3:6-9* clearly explains the covenant or the foundation on which we stand to inherit all of the blessings that salvation brings.

> ⁶ *Even as Abraham believed God, and it was accounted to him for righteousness.*
> ⁷ *Know ye therefore that they which are of faith, the same are the children of Abraham.*
> ⁸ *And the scripture, foreseeing that God would justify the heathen through faith, preached before the gospel unto Abraham, saying, In thee shall all nations be blessed.*
> ⁹ *So then they which be of faith are blessed with faithful Abraham.*
>
> *Galatians 3:6-9*

Our justification as believers is in our faith that Christ and the work of Calvary has truly reconciled, restored and reformed us with God. Justification brings peace with God an gives us access to God by grace. It gives us joy in tribulation, it gives us the right to share in and enjoy the love of God in our hearts. The Holy Spirit is given to us by the Father and we are saved from the wrath of God.

The work of salvation does not just stop at redeeming your soul from eternal damnation, if goes further and restores you to your place of glory which God intended for you at the very beginning of time. God desires for all men to prosper and enjoy the benefits of His blessings, but most believers stop short at the work of the cross and have no knowledge or limited knowledge of what is embedded in this precious gift of salvation.

How do I claim the blessing of Abraham?

We often say Abraham's blessings belong to us, how do you then lay claim to these blessings if they really belong to you? This blessing of Abraham is a transferable blessing. It moves from generation to generation through all that embrace the blessing and the channel (Jesus) through which it flows in this modern times. Let us look at some steps we can follow to make the blessings become a reality.

1. *Salvation*

As we have said, Salvation is the beginning of the promise of God in this generation we live in.

[14] That the blessing of Abraham might come on the Gentiles through Jesus Christ; that we might receive the promise of the Spirit through faith.

Galatians 3:14

Galatians 3:14 makes clear that Abraham's blessings come through Jesus. Salvation paved way for you to the receive the Spirit of God, that we may have God dwell on earth and fulfil His will on earth through us. It gave God the legal right to reside on earth and interfere in earthly matters through the believer. Without salvation we cannot receive the promise of the Spirit. The Spirit of God is the power that makes the blessing a reality in our lives.

2. Faith

Faith towards God is one of the foundations of Christianity. Without the exercising of faith we cannot obtain promises from God. Without expressing our beliefs in the written and spoken Word of God and acting like the Word of God is true, we will not see great results. The blessings of Abraham come by faith and not by works. Abraham was considered a righteous man because he believed God and not because he did anything or any works to earn being righteous before God. However, the expression of his belief in God demanded an action, the sacrifice of his son. Remember, faith without works is dead. It is God who imputes righteousness on anyone. Simply put, you cannot earn righteousness through your works or acts. Abraham believed before acting.

3. Understand the Power of the Covenant

Understanding the promise and the covenant the promise is based on is very important for any believer who wants to take dominion on earth and live a victorious life. Your inheritance in God is founded on the fact that through Jesus you can be all things. Abraham had faith in God which paved way for Jesus to come to the world and bless every family with salvation.

We are all children of God by faith in Jesus (*Galatians* 3:26). If you are of Christ then you are Abraham's seed and heir according to the promise (*Galatians* 3:29). These scriptures have a huge significance in the life of any believer.

Some of us do not understand nor appreciate the test Abraham passed when he was asked to sacrifice Isaac in *Genesis 22:1-19*, Abraham had two sons, Ishmael and Isaac, the first was a by product of his fleshly desires by a bondwoman and the latter is the product of the promise from the free woman. (*Galatians 4:7-31*), God asked him to sacrifice the promise and Abraham obeyed without a shadow of doubt, reflecting God in a sense. The bondwoman and her child had to be cast out because they had no part in the inheritance with the free woman and her child of promise. In the same way, sin and its bondage has to be cast out from the life of a man to enable such to receive the promise.

God could use Abraham because as God did not withhold His own Son Jesus from coming to save the world, Abraham was willing to give up the promise he had waited so long for. Isaac.

Adoption by The Promise

As children of God we have been redeemed from the law by faith and have received the Spirit of adoption as sons of God.

> [5] *To redeem them that were under the law, that we might receive the adoption of sons.*
> [6] *And because ye are sons, God hath sent forth the Spirit of his Son into your hearts, crying, Abba, Father.*
> [7] *Wherefore thou art no more a servant, but a son; and if a son, then an heir of God through Christ.*
>
> Galatians 4:5-7

We are no more servants to God but sons and daughters. We are no longer Godless in this world. His Spirit in us gives us the right to call Him Father.

> [14] *For as many as are led by the Spirit of God, they are the sons of God.*
> [15] *For ye have not received the spirit of bondage again to fear; but ye have received the Spirit of adoption, whereby we cry, Abba, Father.*
> [16] *The Spirit itself beareth witness with our spirit, that we are the children of God:*
> [17] *And if children, then heirs; heirs of God, and joint-heirs with Christ; if so be that we suffer with him, that we may be also glorified together.*
>
> *Romans 8:14-17*

I can authoritatively say that every single word written in the Bible, every word uttered by God concerning you is yours to inherit. Do not short change yourself.

The Bible is God's will and testament to you. It has laid out all that God has said concerning you and what He has prepared for you. I guess you will ask yourself why would I refer to the Bible as a will and testament? Prior to the life and death of Jesus, God had been putting everything together, pronouncing, declaring and establishing. The inheritance kept getting bigger and bigger until it was ripe enough to be obtained.

Jesus died on the cross to perfect the inheritance in God and when He declared *"it is finished"* in (*John 19:30*), He did not just want you to possess earthly treasures. He wants you to have an eternal inheritance. The death of Jesus makes the Bible His will, detailing His wishes and desires for us. As long as you believe in Him and are of Him, everything He has promised would be fulfilled. He is truly the mediator that makes adoption possible to all.

> [15] *And for this cause he is the mediator of the new testament, that by means of death, for the redemption of the transgressions that were under the first testament, they which are called might receive the promise of eternal inheritance.*
> [16] *For where a testament is, there must also of necessity be the death*

of the testator.
¹⁷ For a testament is of force after men are dead: otherwise it is of no strength at all while the testator liveth.

Hebrews 9:15-17

Many believers have not come into the full realisation of what it is to be a co-heir with Christ Jesus and an heir of the only living God. They have no clue as to what their inheritance is. This is the one reason why there are many believers walking and living below average, intimidated by life, harassed and oppressed by circumstances, fearful and lacking confidence in Christ that has made all things perfect. It is time to wake up.

My Inheritance

Sometime back I came across a picture on the Internet. It was a kitten looking into the mirror, and all the kitten could see was a lion. It saw itself as a lion and not as a cat. Hilarious it may seem, it paints a picture of how believers should envision themselves. Jesus has given us the right to be called children of God. I do not think that we fully understand what it means to have the Spirit of God dwelling in us.

Well, I am not going to assume that I know how you visualize God in your mind's eye. It is the knowledge you have of God that will determine how you perceive yourself. My aim here is to help you understand your inheritance and hope in Christ Jesus.

- God has blessed you with all spiritual blessings in heavenly places in Christ. (*Ephesians 1:3*).

- You are chosen by God and made holy and blameless before Him, even before the foundations of the world. (*Ephesians 1:4*).

- You have a life of immortality in Christ as He has abolished death and brought life through the light of the gospel. *(2 Timothy 1:10).*

- Your inheritance is incorruptible, undefiled and does not fade away. Reserved in heaven for you, which is kept by God through faith unto salvation. *(1 Peter 1:4-5).*

- Your inheritance has sealed you with the Holy Spirit of God which has sealed you unto redemption, until the fullness of the Spirit is received and the fullness of redemption complete *(Ephesians 1:14, 2 Corinthians 1:22).*

- Your inheritance has brought you redemption through the blood of Jesus, forgiveness of sins according to the riches of His grace, which has translated you from the power of darkness into the kingdom of God. You are an heir of light, darkness no longer has power or authority over you. *(Colossians 1:13-14)*

- Your inheritance has brought you near to Christ. Prior to believing and accepting the redeeming power of the blood of Jesus, you were a stranger to the covenant of promise, you had no hope and was without a God in this world, but you are justified by the blood of Jesus to enter fully into your inheritance. *(Ephesians 2:11-13).*

- Your inheritance makes you a fellow citizen with the saints and the household of God. Being no more a stranger, you have direct access to the Father. Jesus became your peace and broke the wall of partition between you and God *(Ephesians 3:14).*

- It makes available in you the indwelling of Christ in your heart that you are rooted and grounded in love and your inner man is strengthened with power by the Spirit (*Ephesians 3:16-17*).

If you take your time to further study the scriptures, you will discover more of what you stand to inherit. You are not in a purposeless or meaningless journey in life. Jesus gives your life purpose here on earth and a meaningful life after death.

Possessing My Inheritance

Now you know who you are in Christ Jesus and have a better understanding of what took place on the cross that has placed you in the position of a heavenly child and a heir of the most High God. You should now have a clearer picture of your identity and identity gives you purpose. It is now up to you to put your inheritance into good use. Remember, an inheritance not claimed remains dormant and the possessor can die of the very thing the inheritance provides deliverance from. This inheritance in Christ has in it the inherent power of dominion and authority. What do I mean by this? Let us take a look at dominion and authority.

Dominion

Dominion is defined as the power or right of governing and controlling; sovereign authority. Going back to the book of the beginning in *Genesis 1:26*; God was in the act of creation and at this point He created man (*Adam*) in His image and likeness and gave him dominion over all other creation. *In His image and likeness* means resemblance in outward form, physical likeness (*Romans 1:20*). Man is the representation of God, he is the glory of God (*1 Corinthians 11:7*). He created man in the image of gods and breathe life into him by His Spirit. You therefore are not a descendant of an ape or monkey, and you definitely did not evolve from uncertainty. Your heritage is certain.

Science would like you to believe that you evolved and have postulated some very interesting theories all in a bid to explain the unknown, but common sense would tell that like begat like, apes cannot begat man and neither can man begat an ape even if they cross breed. In *Genesis 1:20-25* we see that everything that was created was created after its kind, if creatures evolved from one degree to another there will be chaos on earth.

> ²⁰ *And God said, Let the waters bring forth abundantly the moving creature that hath life, and fowl that may fly above the earth in the open firmament of heaven.*
> ²¹ *And God created great whales, and every living creature that moveth, which the waters brought forth abundantly, after their kind, and every winged fowl after his kind: and God saw that it was good.*
> ²² *And God blessed them, saying, Be fruitful, and multiply, and fill the waters in the seas, and let fowl multiply in the earth.*
> ²³ *And the evening and the morning were the fifth day.*
> ²⁴ *And God said, Let the earth bring forth the living creature after his kind, cattle, and creeping thing, and beast of the earth after his kind: and it was so.*
> ²⁵ *And God made the beast of the earth after his kind, and cattle after their kind, and every thing that creepeth upon the earth after his kind: and God saw that it was good.*
>
> *Genesis 1:20-25*

I certainly know that apes cannot birth or evolve into intellectual beings with a free will and a conscience. An ape is not a free moral agent, how then would God give you dominion over all creation (*ape inclusive*) when you are an ape yourself or a product of an ape? You definitely can do better than that. Butterflies do not evolve into eagles just because they have wings and even if they so wished and meerkats do not evolve into Cheetahs either. Frogs do not turn into princes, even if it were a fairy tale.

God said man should have dominion over everything, over all the earth.

> [26] And God said, Let us make man in our image, after our likeness: and let them have dominion over the fish of the sea, and over the fowl of the air, and over the cattle, and over all the earth, and over every creeping thing that creepeth upon the earth.
> [27] So God created man in his own image, in the image of God created he him; male and female created he them.
> [28] And God blessed them, and God said unto them, Be fruitful, and multiply, and replenish the earth, and subdue it: and have dominion over the fish of the sea, and over the fowl of the air, and over every living thing that moveth upon the earth.
>
> *Genesis 1:26-28*

God blessed man (*male and female*) to be fruitful, multiply, replenish the earth, subdue it and have dominion over every living thing that moved upon the earth (*verse 28*). When Adam and Eve sinned, man lost his dominating status, and we can see from the way we live now, dominion is something that is farfetched in the mind of man. Man originally was created to rule over everything, the entire earth but the reverse appears to be the case. David in *Psalm 8* resounds this when he said in *verse 6 "thou made him to have dominion over the works of thy hands, You have put all things under his feet"*. How much dominion are you exercising in your life today?

Authority

Authority is inherent in dominion. Authority gives you right to control, command or determine outcomes, have legal power to enforce, to rule, influence, power to exact obedience, confidence, strength and supremacy. Authority or otherwise power is not something that we exercise in our daily life, some believers even live in abject fear of everything that can be feared. The original plan is not what we see today, the one who has the power to dominate is the one being dominated. How comical, man is now the underdog, the freedom to communicate freely with God is lost, righteousness and true holiness is a phantom, the full dominion over all things, the full power to do good, power over satan, perfect health and all the benefits of a perfect union with God. God consciousness and friendship with God was all lost.

I thank God that He sent Jesus Christ to reconcile us to our God, Maker, Friend and Father. Man has been miserable since his departure from grace, but all the power we need to take dominion in life is in Christ.

> *[18] And Jesus came and spake unto them, saying, All power is given unto me in heaven and in earth.*
> *[19] Go ye therefore, and teach all nations, baptizing them in the name of the Father, and of the Son, and of the Holy Ghost:*
> *[20] Teaching them to observe all things whatsoever I have commanded you: and, lo, I am with you always, even unto the end of the world. Amen.*
>
> *Matthew 28:18-20*

Jesus speaking to His disciples said *"all power is given to me in heaven and in earth"*, and Jesus has given us the authority to continue all that He came to the earth to do. This authority is the threefold authority, the authority of God the Father, God the Son and God the Holy Spirit.

God highly exalted Jesus for His obedience and selflessness on the cross.

> *[9] Wherefore God also hath highly exalted him, and given him a name which is above every name:*
> *[10] That at the name of Jesus every knee should bow, of things in heaven, and things in earth, and things under the earth;*
> *[11] And that every tongue should confess that Jesus Christ is Lord, to*

the glory of God the Father.
¹² Wherefore, my beloved, as ye have always obeyed, not as in my presence only, but now much more in my absence, work out your own salvation with fear and trembling.

Philippians 2:9-12

In *Luke 9:1*, we find that Jesus empowers His twelve disciples with the power and authority over all devils, to cure diseases, to preach the kingdom of God and to heal the sick. It is therefore imperative that to live this life you need to be empowered.

¹⁹ Look, I have given you authority over all the power of the enemy, and you can walk among snakes and scorpions and crush them. Nothing will injure you.

Luke 10:19 (NLT)

You have been given the legal power to enforce, to rule, influence, power to exact obedience, confidence, mastery, strength and supremacy to destroy the works of satan when needed.

¹³ Thou shalt tread upon the lion and adder: the young lion and the dragon shalt thou trample under feet.

Psalm 91:13

Power is given to you because you need to understand that those waging war against you are intelligent and organized. Jesus rejoices in *Luke 10:21* because He was able to reveal to us the will of the Father, which is for us to triumph over the enemy and to glorify His name. He tells of how satan fell from heaven like lightning signifying victory for all that believe. Jesus made a pronouncement on the church in the gospel of Matthew.

¹⁸ And I say also unto thee, That thou art Peter, and upon this rock I will build my church; and the gates of hell shall not prevail against it.
¹⁹ And I will give unto thee the keys of the kingdom of heaven: and

whatsoever thou shalt bind on earth shall be bound in heaven: and whatsoever thou shalt loose on earth shall be loosed in heaven.

Matthew 16:18-19

All authority has been handed over to you, and the key to the empowerment is the name of Jesus

¹³ And whatsoever ye shall ask in my name, that will I do, that the Father may be glorified in the Son.
¹⁴ If ye shall ask any thing in my name, I will do it.

John 14:13-14

Jesus says whatever you ask in His name, that will He do, that the Father may be glorified. That is all the assurance you will ever need in the place of prayer. The only thing that can stop you now is you, because you have heaven's endorsement. Jesus has released the Spirit that fills you with power from heaven (*Luke 24:49*) so you can exercise heavenly authority. The devil does not want you to come into full realisation of who you are and the power available to you as a child of God but God has done a great work by deciding to live in you.

⁴ Ye are of God, little children, and have overcome them: because greater is he that is in you, than he that is in the world.

1 John 4:4

You are an overcomer because you are a child of God. Elisha could not have said it in clearer words when he said to his servant in (*2 kings 6:16*) *"fear not for they that are with us are more than they that are with them"*. There is a heavenly force that supports us on the earth.

²⁰ Which he wrought in Christ, when he raised him from the dead, and set him at his own right hand in the heavenly places,
²¹ Far above all principality, and power, and might, and dominion, and every name that is named, not only in this world, but also in that which is to come:

²² And hath put all things under his feet, and gave him to be the head over all things to the church,

Ephesians 1:20-22

Jesus being seated in heavenly places has also raised you up together with Him and made you sit with Him in heavenly places. So even though we are conscious of the existence of the forces of darkness, they are no threat to us because we are seated with Jesus far above these principalities and powers.

⁶ And hath raised us up together, and made us sit together in heavenly places in Christ Jesus:

Ephesians 2:6

God has not given you the spirit of fear. Fear is of the devil to make you feel incapable of doing anything and enjoying all that God has made available to you but God has given you the Spirit of love, power and of sound mind. (*2 Timothy 1:7*). You have not received the spirit of bondage to fear again, you can cry, Abba Father, recognising God as your source and only source of help at any given time.

By now, you may be wondering how you fit all this information into your day-to-day living, to ensure that you constantly live a victorious life over all the wiles and fiery darts that the enemy throws at you. Let us examine two key areas we need to have a good understanding of in order to live this life of victory. These are 'Our understanding of the Word of God' and 'Our understanding of the Holy Spirit'.

Chapter Summary

In Abraham's days, covenants were used to seal an
agreement to make it unbreakable

Abraham was God's responsibility and obedience was
Abraham's obligation

An inheritance not claimed remains dormant and
the possessor can die of the very thing the inheritance
provides deliverance from

The only thing that can stop you now is you

Chapter 5

Understanding the Word of God

*L*et us settle this fact before we delve into this topic. The Word of God is something that is inexhaustible. It is too wide and too deep that devoting volumes and volumes to the topic will not allow us to say all that can be said. Most preachers of the Word of God refer to it, many authors refer to it in their work, like I have done in this book. We come across many writings but what exactly is the WORD of God?

The book of John 1:1-5 gives a fitting illustration:

> *¹ In the beginning was the Word, and the Word was with God, and the Word was God.*
> *² The same was in the beginning with God.*
> *³ All things were made by him; and without him was not any thing made that was made.*
> *⁴ In him was life; and the life was the light of men.*
> *⁵ And the light shineth in darkness; and the darkness comprehended it not.*
>
> *John 1:1-5*

This is a very well known scripture for anyone who has been in Christianity for any length of time. So, let us break it down to gain more understanding of what God is saying through these verses of scripture.

In the beginning was the Word, and the Word was with God and the Word was God. John 1:1

If God existed before the beginning as we know it, His Word must have existed with Him. Can you imagine someone without impediments in their speech existing without any words? Words are the very expression of life. Words signify the presence of life and have personality. The Word referred to in this verse is Jesus Christ.

> [13] *And he was clothed with a vesture dipped in blood: and his name is called The Word of God.*
>
> *Revelation 19:13*

Jesus is the Word which was at the beginning, and Jesus was with God and Jesus is God. Jesus is an eternal being just like God the Father and the Holy Spirit. He is one of the members of the divine trinity. He is described as Alpha and Omega, the Almighty, the one that lives and is alive forevermore.

> [8] *I am Alpha and Omega, the beginning and the ending, saith the Lord, which is, and which was, and which is to come, the Almighty.* [18] *I am he that liveth, and was dead; and, behold, I am alive for evermore, Amen; and have the keys of hell and of death.*
>
> *Revelation 1:8,18*

If Jesus lives forever, it means His Words must be living forever. His words were living when he spoke them, they are living now and they will be living when future generations hear them.

63 It is the spirit that quickeneth; the flesh profiteth nothing: the words that I speak unto you, they are spirit, and they are life.

Jesus's words are spirit and spirits do not die, it means His words carry the same power today, that they did when He originally spoke them. As His Words are also life, it means when His Words get to someone today that requires life, the Words of God will be life to them. God's Word never returns to Him without accomplishing what it was sent to accomplish. The Word of God will forever remain relevant.

What am I saying? The Word that was in the beginning is the same Word that is available today. Its potency has not reduced for those who can search it out. You do not have to go from pillar to post searching for God in temples made with hands. All you need to do is to search for Him where He may be found. In His Word, His Words have been alive all these years and have responded favourably to many who called on the Word. Your call will produce the same results.

The same was in the beginning with God, all things were made by Him, and without Him nothing was not made that was made. John 1:2-3

Was He really in the beginning with God? Were all things really made by Him? How else can we answer these questions without asking Him (*The Word of God*)? Let us see what He has to say Himself about these questions.

14 ......These things saith the Amen, the faithful and true witness, the beginning of the creation of God;

Revelation 3:14

Jesus calls Himself, the beginning of the creation of God.

This means that without Jesus, nothing else was made and anything that was made was made for Him.

> *16 For by him were all things created, that are in heaven, and that are in earth, visible and invisible, whether they be thrones, or dominions, or principalities, or powers: all things were created by him, and for him:*
> *17 And he is before all things, and by him all things consist.*
>
> *Colossians 1:16-17*

God the Father, has given us the opportunity many times over and over again, to recognise Jesus as the preeminent one. Despite this, people still reject Him not wanting to believe Him but rather to believe a lie. God has been active in past generations revealing Jesus but people have consistently rejected Him. See what Apostle Paul through the Spirit says in *Hebrews 1:1-3*:

> *1 IN MANY separate revelations [each of which set forth a portion of the Truth] and in different ways God spoke of old to [our] forefathers in and by the prophets,*
> *2 [But] in the last of these days He has spoken to us in [the person of a] Son, Whom He appointed Heir and lawful Owner of all things, also by and through Whom He created the worlds and the reaches of space and the ages of time [He made, produced, built, operated, and arranged them in order].*
> *3 He is the sole expression of the glory of God [the Light-being, the out-raying or radiance of the divine], and He is the perfect imprint and very image of [God's] nature, upholding and maintaining and guiding and propelling the universe by His mighty word of power. When He had by offering Himself accomplished our cleansing of sins and riddance of guilt, He sat down at the right hand of the divine Majesty on high,*
>
> *Hebrews 1:1-3 (AMP)*

Any revelation of the glory of God anybody has ever had is really a revelation of Jesus, the sole expression of His glory. What do I mean by this? When someone sees you, they have not really seen the real you, what they have seen is the physical container that represents you. Jesus is the physical container of the Godhead. There is no way you can see the glory of God without seeing Jesus and there is no way you can see Jesus without seeing His Word. Even in the days of Moses the great prophet of God, he spoke about Jesus, yet the people did not accept Jesus when he showed up in the flesh. The Bible is the story of Jesus, the Word of God captured in readable form for preservation and transference to generations unborn.

> [46] *For had ye believed Moses, ye would have believed me; for he wrote of me.*
> [47] *But if ye believe not his writings, how shall ye believe my words?*
>
> *John 5:46-47*

Everything God created, He created with words. The same Words that were spoken during creation can still create for you in any area in which you desire it to. If things are desolate around you, use the same word to create your Eden.

> ***In Him was life and the life was the light of men, and the light shines in the darkness, but the darkness has not understood it. John 1:4-5 (NIV).***

The presence of life always produces light. Jesus is the Light pronounced to put darkness in its place in *Genesis 1:3-4*:

> [3] *And God said, Let there be light: and there was light.*
> [4] *And God saw the light, that it was good: and God divided the light from the darkness.*
>
> *Genesis 1:3-4*

Darkness can never overcome or overshadow the Word

of God. The Word of God spoils principalities and powers (*Colossians 2:15*). Jesus is the true Light and anyone who follows Him will not walk in darkness, but will have the light of life (*John 8:12*). The power of life in Christ Jesus will always set free from the power of sin and death. This life is the same eternal life that we have when we accept Jesus as the Word of God.

> *The Word was made flesh and dwelt among us, we beheld His glory, the glory of the only begotten of the Father, full of grace and truth. John 1:14*

How was the Word made flesh? How did the Word so great in glory take on a form, tangible in nature, that man could relate to? I am sure many people like Mary would be thinking in their hearts, how can this happen? That answer is very simple. It is the same answer the angel that visited Mary gave her.

> [35] *And the angel answered and said unto her, The Holy Ghost shall come upon thee, and the power of the Highest shall overshadow thee: therefore also that holy thing which shall be born of thee shall be called the Son of God.*
>
> *Luke 1:35*

He was conceived by the Holy Spirit, the incorruptible and uncontaminated Spirit of God. He was the first-born of God in human flesh. God through Mary was showing that in future, He will begin to live in bodies of flesh by the power of the Holy Spirit.

> [4] *But when the fulness of the time was come, God sent forth his Son, made of a woman, made under the law,*
>
> *Galatians 4:4*

Things of God can take on bodily form. Do not give up on

your dream? The power of the Spirit can overshadow you and cause something great to come out of nothing.

Knowing what we now know about the Word of God, there is a disposition we need to have towards His Words in order to get results in our everyday life. Let us consider a few of these.

1.   *Believe the Word is greater than your Mind*

It is difficult to comprehend the sonship of Jesus Christ with human intelligence. Being a woman, Mary had to ask, *'how can these things be?'*. Even if others thought she was lying about being impregnated by the Spirit of God, at least she would know herself, that she was still a virgin yet pregnant. Things of God do not come from the head, they come from the heart. God is able to do things that your head cannot analyse or find a logical connection for.

> *[13] Which things also we speak, not in the words which man's wisdom teacheth, but which the Holy Ghost teacheth; comparing spiritual things with spiritual.*
> *[14] But the natural man receiveth not the things of the Spirit of God: for they are foolishness unto him: neither can he know them, because they are spiritually discerned.*
>
> *1 Corinthians 2:13-14*

The Word of God can cause transformations to happen in your environment that no human law will be able to explain. So do not be limited in your thinking. All things are possible to the one that believes. The natural man receives not the things of the Spirit of God, for they are foolishness unto him, neither can he know them because they are spiritually discerned. It took me a while to come into full understanding of this God, Saviour, Brother and Friend that Jesus is. This understanding totally changed my perception of life.

2. Believe in the power of the Word and its flawlessness

The Word of God is powerful and sharp. Remember the Word of God is a person. "*Jesus*" To believe in the power of the Word is to believe that Jesus is able. He has more power than your mind can conceive. Look at these descriptions of the Word of God.

> [12] *For the word of God is quick, and powerful, and sharper than any twoedged sword, piercing even to the dividing asunder of soul and spirit, and of the joints and marrow, and is a discerner of the thoughts and intents of the heart.*
>
> *Hebrews 4:12*

> [6] *The words of the LORD are pure words: as silver tried in a furnace of earth, purified seven times.*
>
> *Psalm 12:6*

> [4] *For the word of the LORD is right; and all his works are done in truth.* [5] *He loveth righteousness and judgment: the earth is full of the goodness of the LORD.* [6] *By the word of the LORD were the heavens made; and all the host of them by the breath of his mouth.*
>
> *Psalm 33:4-6*

> [20] *He sent his word, and healed them, and delivered them from their destructions.*
>
> *Psalm 107:20*

The power of God's Word is the ultimate power for a number of reasons. Firstly, there is no one greater than Him and this eliminates the chances of someone greater than Him changing His Words. Secondly, God's word is flawless. Unfortunately, some people mistaken their lack of understanding for inaccuracies in God. It is important to understand the certainty of the Word of God as everything in life is anchored on the Word. The word of God has been tried and tested seven times and has no blemish or error in it.

⁹ For he spake, and it was done; he commanded, and it stood fast.

Psalm 33:9

⁷ The law of the LORD is perfect, converting the soul: the testimony of the LORD is sure, making wise the simple.

Psalm 19:7

When you look at the entire Bible, one thing that is evident is the fact that everything God has spoken is gradually being fulfilled in the appropriate time. Who can annul what the Lord has purposed? If His hand is stretched out who can turn it back? (*Isaiah 14:24,26-27*). When God made a promise to Abraham, He swore by Himself since He had no one greater by whom to swear.

¹³ For when God made promise to Abraham, because he could swear by no greater, he sware by himself,

Hebrews 6:13

¹⁶ Seek out of the book of the Lord and read: not one of these [details of prophecy] shall fail, none shall want and lack her mate [in fulfillment]. For the mouth [of the Lord] has commanded, and His Spirit has gathered them.

Isaiah 34:16 (AMP)

If God has made a pronouncement, it will stand no matter what. His Words will never change. As they were in the very beginning, so it is this very day. Be rest assured that His Word will not fail you as long as you believe in them. *God is not a man that He should lie neither is He of human descent that He will change His mind, whatever He says, you can be rest assured that He will do it. Has He spoken and shall He not make it good? (Numbers 23:19-20)*. Balaam in *verse 20* said to Balak that the Lord *"has commanded me to bless Israel, He has blessed and I cannot reverse it or qualify it."* This is again restated in *1 Samuel 15:29* by Samuel *"the strength of Israel*

Page | 45

will not lie nor repent for He is not a man that He should repent".

> [18] *This was so that, by two unchangeable things [His promise and His oath] in which it is impossible for God ever to prove false or deceive us, we who have fled [to Him] for refuge might have mighty indwelling strength and strong encouragement to grasp and hold fast the hope appointed for us and set before [us].*

Hebrews 6:18 (AMP)

Build up your confidence in the authenticity of His word. I am sure that by now the Word of God should be taking on a new meaning to you. I pray that these words that I have shared with you will drive you into greater depths in your search for more of God from His Word.

Chapter Summary

The Word of God is something that is inexhaustible.

Words signify the presence of life and have personality.

To believe in the power of the Word is to believe that Jesus is able. He has more power than your mind can conceive.

Chapter 6

Understanding the Holy Spirit

*T*he Holy Spirit is the Spirit of God. He is the third person in the Holy Trinity. He is not an indistinct intangible force. He is a personality with great intellect, mental power and emotions with access to the mind of God.

> *[11] For what man knoweth the things of a man, save the spirit of man which is in him? even so the things of God knoweth no man, but the Spirit of God.*
>
> *1 Corinthians 2:11*

This is a very interesting scripture because it compares the relationship a man's spirit has with a man to the relationship the Holy Spirit has with God. It is not possible to separate your spirit from you and it is not possible to separate your mind from you. You and your spirit are one. The same thing applies to God and the Holy Spirit, both of them are one. You cannot separate the Holy Spirit from God. The Holy Spirit is the Spirit of Jesus. Wherever the Spirit of God is, God is. The same way you can be in one place physically, yet have your mind on something thousand of miles away, God can be in one place, Heaven, and have His Spirit manifesting miles and miles away, Earth. When you think about it this way, you realise that it is not a difficult concept to understand the workings and operations of the Spirit of God.

The Holy Spirit is a personality that experiences the same sort of feelings that we as people experience. He can be grieved, His operations can be quenched. He does not go where He is not wanted and many more. Let us see some of these traits in the Bible that demonstrate that He is a personality.

He can be grieved

To grieve is really to make upset or uncomfortable. The Holy Spirit is very sensitive and can be grieved. He can be grieved in different ways.

> [30] *And grieve not the holy Spirit of God, whereby ye are sealed unto the day of redemption.*
>
> *Ephesians 4:30*

Grieving the Holy Spirit usually comes from the things we think and do. For most people, we reject Him in our minds before we reject Him openly. Because He knows what is in our minds, many inward things not apparent to others on the outside can actually grieve Him. Our self-justifications, evil thoughts, indulgent thoughts of pride and the likes will fall into this category.

He can be quenched

> [19] *Quench not the Spirit.*
>
> *1 Thessalonians 5:19*

Quenching the Spirit is the result of consistent grieving. Most of us do not mind being upset by those we love every now and again but if this continues consistently, we would usually withdraw and avoid the source of pain and go where you are celebrated.

He can be blasphemed

³¹ Wherefore I say unto you, All manner of sin and blasphemy shall be forgiven unto men: but the blasphemy against the Holy Ghost shall not be forgiven unto men.

Matthew 12:31

Blaspheming means to curse or speak irreverently or profanely about God. It is counted as an unforgiveable sin because the Holy Spirit is the power of God to make things happen. If you have openly rejected Him, then what power will cause the transformation in you?.

He has forms

⁴ Now there are diversities of gifts, but the same Spirit.
⁵ And there are differences of administrations, but the same Lord.
⁶ And there are diversities of operations, but it is the same God which worketh all in all.
⁷ But the manifestation of the Spirit is given to every man to profit withal.

1 Corinthians 12:4-7

The Spirit of God can manifest in different ways. Remember, God took on the form of a man in Jesus. Throughout the Bible, we see the Holy Spirit manifesting in different forms. The Holy Spirit can choose to manifest in whatever form He desires. The form He chooses is not something we control. Even though the Holy Spirit appears in different forms, there is no form favoured above the other. Let us look at some forms of the Spirit of God in scriptures.

The Holy Spirit as a Dove

16 And Jesus, when he was baptized, went up straightway out of the water: and, lo, the heavens were opened unto him, and HE SAW THE SPIRIT OF GOD DESCENDING LIKE A DOVE, and lighting upon him:

Matthew 3:16

The Holy Spirit as Wind

2And suddenly there came a sound from heaven AS OF A RUSHING MIGHTY WIND, and it filled all the house where they were sitting. 3And there appeared unto them cloven tongues like as of fire, and it sat upon each of them.
4And they were all filled with the Holy Ghost, and began to speak with other tongues, as the Spirit gave them utterance.

Acts 2:2-4

The Holy Spirit as Breath

7 And the LORD God formed man of the dust of the ground, and breathed into his nostrils THE BREATH OF LIFE; and man became a living soul.

Genesis 2:7

29 Thou hidest thy face, they are troubled: thou takest away their breath, they die, and return to their dust.
30 Thou sendest forth thy spirit, they are created: and thou renewest the face of the earth.

Psalm 104:29-30

He has gifts

In each believer is deposited the potential to manifest gifts of the Holy Spirit of God. The Holy Spirit will work through everyone that believes and yields to Him. There are various gifts of the Holy Spirit.

⁴ Now there are diversities of gifts, but the same Spirit.

⁷ But the manifestation of the Spirit is given to every man to profit withal.

⁸ For to one is given by the Spirit the word of wisdom; to another the word of knowledge by the same Spirit;

⁹ To another faith by the same Spirit; to another the gifts of healing by the same Spirit;

¹⁰ To another the working of miracles; to another prophecy; to another discerning of spirits; to another divers kinds of tongues; to another the interpretation of tongues:

¹¹ But all these worketh that one and the selfsame Spirit, dividing to every man severally as he will.

1 Corinthians 12:4,7-12

All of these gifts enable believers effectively carry out the purpose of God here on earth. How do you get these gifts? Do they come freely? Is there something I must do to get these gifts? The answer to these questions is yes. While the gifts are available to all, you still need to make the call to have them available to you. Even though you have money in a bank account, there is still a process you will need to go through to withdraw the money and enjoy the benefit of spending it. The gifts of the Spirit are almost similar to this. You need to get this active desire and covet the gifts of the spirit for them to manifest in your life. The baptism of the Holy Spirit is the primary vehicle through which an overflowing of the gifts comes to the believer.

The Baptism of the Holy Spirit

Firstly, in answering the above questions, you do not have to work for the gift of the Spirit to come upon you. The baptism comes freely to all believers but it is important for a believer to seek to be baptised because the baptism of the Holy Spirit is the outpouring of the power of God.

⁸ But ye shall receive power, after that the Holy Ghost is come upon you: and ye shall be witnesses unto me both in Jerusalem, and in all Judaea, and in Samaria, and unto the uttermost part of the earth.

Acts 1:8

He quickens the innate gifts deposited in you to begin to manifest. The Holy Spirit empowers you to be able to speak the spiritual language othrwise known as speaking in tongues. Look at what happened when this scripture in *Acts 1 verse 8* was fulfilled.

> *¹ And when the day of Pentecost was fully come, they were all with one accord in one place.*
> *² And suddenly there came a sound from heaven as of a rushing mighty wind, and it filled all the house where they were sitting.*
> *³ And there appeared unto them cloven tongues like as of fire, and it sat upon each of them.*
> *⁴ And they were all filled with the Holy Ghost, and began to speak with other tongues, as the Spirit gave them utterance.*

Acts 2:1-4

Paul in *1 Corinthians 13:1* refers to speaking in tongues as the tongues of angels, it is a sign to them that do not believe and not for believers because it clearly signifies that you have received the Holy Spirit. Speaking in tongues is like your receipt for being baptised. It is very important to receive this baptism because it is a prayer language necessary for personal prayers, intercession and edification. It is the power that God promised all believers.

Without the power of the Holy Spirit that comes through the baptism, you are spiritually vulnerable. It is another "tool" available to Christians because through it, you build up yourself in faith. This does not mean God cannot use you without the baptism nor does it mean you are not saved. The only experience required in the New Testament for anyone to make heaven is the Salvation Experience.

> *²⁰ But you, beloved, build yourselves up [founded] on your most holy*

faith (make progress, rise like an edifice higher and higher), praying in the Holy Spirit;

Jude 1:20 (AMP)

The first time it was recorded that men spoke in tongues is on the day of Pentecost when the power of the Holy Spirit fell upon the apostles and disciples. Initially, when I heard people speak in tongues, I would wonder what they were doing. I thought they were on another level of acting because I had witnessed all sorts in the name of the power of the Holy Spirit. As time went on, I discovered I had caught what I termed the *"bug"* then but I refused to speak in tongues because I could not be caught in this drama club. I am sure some of you can relate with that, but please let me help you correct that school of thought. Speaking in tongues is a mighty missile available to you that the devil has no understanding of.

When you pray in tongues, you speak God's language. It is like God's code for communicating His will to and through you. You are saying exactly what needs to be said at that given point and the devil does not understand a word you say. When you speak in tongues, you are inspired by the Holy Spirit to speak mysteries, it edifies you and empowers you to adequately praise and thank God (*1 Corinthians 14:2-4, 14-15*). It brings you to the rest and refreshing of God (*Isaiah 28:11-12*).

Unfortunately, the knowledge and essence of the Holy Spirit has been down played in our churches today. An alarming amount of believers do not know the person of the Holy Spirit and thus have little or no relationship with Him.

13 facts about the Holy Spirit

There are many things that can be said about the Holy Spirit but let us look at some facts about Him that will help you boost your understanding of the Holy Spirit. Read these facts over and over again until they enter your heart.

1. *The Holy Spirit is omnipresent.*

   [7] Whither shall I go from thy spirit? or whither shall I flee from thy presence?
   [8] If I ascend up into heaven, thou art there: if I make my bed in hell, behold, thou art there.

   Psalm 139:7-8

2. *He proceeds from God the Father and Son. God reveals Himself through the Holy Spirit.*

   [26] But when the Comforter is come, whom I will send unto you from the Father, even the Spirit of truth, which proceedeth from the Father, he shall testify of me:

   John 15:26

3. *He is the Spirit of holiness.*

   [4] And declared to be the Son of God with power, according to the spirit of holiness, by the resurrection from the dead:

   Romans 1:4

4. *He is the Spirit of adoption that bears witness with us that we are sons of God*

   [15] For ye have not received the spirit of bondage again to fear; but ye have received the Spirit of adoption, whereby we cry, Abba, Father.
   [16] The Spirit itself beareth witness with our spirit, that we are the children of God:

   Romans 8:15-16

5. He is the Spirit of Christ.

⁹ But ye are not in the flesh, but in the Spirit, if so be that the Spirit of God dwell in you. Now if any man have not the Spirit of Christ, he is none of his.

Romans 8:9

6. He is eternal.

¹⁴ How much more shall the blood of Christ, who through the eternal Spirit offered himself without spot to God, purge your conscience from dead works to serve the living God?

Hebrews 9:14

7. He is the Spirit of truth, that is indwelling in all believers.

⁹ But ye are not in the flesh, but in the Spirit, if so be that the Spirit of God dwell in you. Now if any man have not the Spirit of Christ, he is none of his

Romans 8:9

8. He is God the Holy Spirit.

⁴ The spirit of God hath made me, and the breath of the Almighty hath given me life.

Job 33:4

9. He is the source of sanctification and justification.

² Elect according to the foreknowledge of God the Father, through sanctification of the Spirit, unto obedience and sprinkling of the blood of Jesus Christ: Grace unto you, and peace, be multiplied.

1 Peter 1:2

¹⁶ And without controversy great is the mystery of godliness: God was manifest in the flesh, justified in the Spirit, seen of angels, preached unto the Gentiles, believed on in the world, received up into glory.

1 Timothy 3:16

10. *He transforms an unbeliever into a new creature in Christ when there is the acceptance of salvation.*

> ¹⁷ *Therefore if any man be in Christ, he is a new creature: old things are passed away; behold, all things are become new.*
>
> 2 Corinthians 5:17

11. *He is the power behind the miraculous and the casting out of devils*

> ²⁸ *But if I cast out devils by the Spirit of God, then the kingdom of God is come unto you.*
>
> Matthew 12:28

12. *He directs the work of the gospel and is the agent for new birth.*

> ⁵ *Jesus answered, Verily, verily, I say unto thee, Except a man be born of water and of the Spirit, he cannot enter into the kingdom of God.*
> ⁶ *That which is born of the flesh is flesh; and that which is born of the Spirit is spirit.*
> ⁷ *Marvel not that I said unto thee, Ye must be born again.*
> ⁸ *The wind bloweth where it listeth, and thou hearest the sound thereof, but canst not tell whence it cometh, and whither it goeth: so is every one that is born of the Spirit.*
>
> John 3:5-8

13. *He is the Spirit of wisdom and understanding*

> ² *And the spirit of the LORD shall rest upon him, the spirit of wisdom and understanding, the spirit of counsel and might, the spirit of knowledge and of the fear of the LORD;*
>
> Isaiah 11:2

11 things the Holy Spirit does for the believer.

1. *He strengthens the inner man*

[16] That he would grant you, according to the riches of his glory, to be strengthened with might by his Spirit in the inner man;

Ephesians 3:16

2. *He gives spiritual gifts to every believer*

[7] But the manifestation of the Spirit is given to every man to profit withal.

1 Corinthians 12:7

3. *He teaches the believer how to love*

[5] And hope maketh not ashamed; because the love of God is shed abroad in our hearts by the Holy Ghost which is given unto us.

Romans 5:5

4. *He helps to intercede and teaches how to pray the right way and reveals the heart, mind and will of God.*

[26] Likewise the Spirit also helpeth our infirmities: for we know not what we should pray for as we ought: but the Spirit itself maketh intercession for us with groanings which cannot be uttered.

[27] And he that searcheth the hearts knoweth what is the mind of the Spirit, because he maketh intercession for the saints according to the will of God.

Romans 8:26-27

5. *He teaches a believer to be obedient*

[22] Seeing ye have purified your souls in obeying the truth through the Spirit unto unfeigned love of the brethren, see that ye love one another with a pure heart fervently:

1 Peter 1:22

6. *He teaches all things and reminds the believer of all things.*

   [26] But the Comforter, which is the Holy Ghost, whom the Father will send in my name, he shall teach you all things, and bring all things to your remembrance, whatsoever I have said unto you.

   John 14:26

7. *He is the source of our hope in Jesus Christ.*

   [5] For we through the Spirit wait for the hope of righteousness by faith.

   Galatians 5:5

8. *He makes the believer flourish and is the source of harvest.*

   [7] Be not deceived; God is not mocked: for whatsoever a man soweth, that shall he also reap.
   [8] For he that soweth to his flesh shall of the flesh reap corruption; but he that soweth to the Spirit shall of the Spirit reap life everlasting.

   Galatians 6:7-8

9. *He gives the believer access to God and changes lives into the image of Christ.*

   [18] But we all, with open face beholding as in a glass the glory of the Lord, are changed into the same image from glory to glory, even as by the Spirit of the Lord.

   2 Corinthians 3:18

10. *The Holy Spirit empowers man to stand in the place of warfare against the kingdom of darkness, He is a weapon that is used against darkness as a believer can lift a standard against satan by the Holy Spirit.*

    [19] So shall they fear the name of the LORD from the west, and his glory from the rising of the sun. When the enemy shall come in like a flood, the Spirit of the LORD shall lift up a standard against him.

    Isaiah 59:19

11. *He searches the mind and thoughts of God*

¹⁰ But God hath revealed them unto us by his Spirit: for the Spirit searcheth all things, yea, the deep things of God.
¹¹ For what man knoweth the things of a man, save the spirit of man which is in him? even so the things of God knoweth no man, but the Spirit of God.
¹² Now we have received, not the spirit of the world, but the spirit which is of God; that we might know the things that are freely given to us of God.

1 Corinthians 2:10-12

¹⁰ Yet to us God has unveiled and revealed them by and through His Spirit, for the [Holy] Spirit searches diligently, exploring and examining everything, even sounding the profound and bottomless things of God (the divine counsels and things hidden and beyond man's scrutiny).

1 Corinthians 2:10 (AMP)

The Holy Spirit is the power that quickens the Word. He is the sword of the Spirit which is the word of God. Jesus said in *John 6:63, "it is the Spirit that quickeneth; the flesh profiteth nothing: the words that I speak they are Spirit and they are life"*, God's words are spirit (*Holy Spirit*) and life (*Jesus Christ*) therefore the word of God comprises of Jesus Christ and the Holy Spirit. They walk and work hand in hand, when the word of God is spoken, the Holy Spirit is at work. They cannot be separated in any way Look at what Paul says in *1 Corinthians 4:20.*

²⁰For the kingdom of God consists of and is based on not talk but power (moral power and excellence of soul).

1 Corinthians 4:20 (AMP)

How do you access or obtain all of these wonderful things? It is through believing in God or having faith in God.

Chapter Summary

It is not possible to separate your spirit from you and it is not possible to separate your mind from you. You and your spirit are one.

The Holy Spirit is a personality that experiences the same sort of feelings that we as people experience.

Without the power of the Holy Spirit that comes through the baptism, you are spiritually vulnerable.

Chapter 7

Understanding this thing called Faith

A life of faith is something you cannot get away from. To enjoy the benefits of being a believer, you must have faith and live a life of faith. You must believe the Bible is the Word of God. Jesus speaking to His disciples in *Matthew 21:21-22* & *Mark 11:22* said;

> *²¹ Jesus answered and said unto them, Verily I say unto you, If ye have faith, and doubt not, ye shall not only do this which is done to the fig tree, but also if ye shall say unto this mountain, Be thou removed, and be thou cast into the sea; it shall be done.*
> *²² And all things, whatsoever ye shall ask in prayer, believing, ye shall receive.*
>
> *Matthew 21:21-22*

> *²²And Jesus answering saith unto them, Have faith in God.*
>
> *Mark 11:22*

So what is this thing called *"FAITH"*? Where else can we go to define faith but the Word of God?

> *¹ NOW FAITH is the assurance (the confirmation, the title deed) of*

the things [we] hope for, being the proof of things [we] do not see and the conviction of their reality [faith perceiving as real fact what is not revealed to the senses].

Faith is the principle of inward and whole hearted confidence, assurance, trust and reliance on God and all that He says in His Word. Faith is what pleases God.

I had always approached faith from a point of difficulty. All I knew from the onset was that faith was a hard thing to get. I thought it was something I could mentally comprehend but every time I heard sermons about faith I knew I did not have the kind of faith spoken about in the Bible. It was worse when I heard about the kind of faith the patriarch Abraham had, unwavering faith, believing in God without entertaining any form of doubt, waiting patiently for the fulfilment of the promise. I knew this was out of my league because every time I prayed, some wavering thought would accompany my Amen. I was ready to buy faith if it were sold. I just did not know where. I even thought I needed deliverance at some point, deliverance from *"doubt"*

I started getting really frustrated and at a point I gave up on the search for faith. I had concluded that I would never find the kind of faith that the Bible spoke about, then I stumbled or properly said, the Holy Spirit led me to the scripture in *Jeremiah 3:22.*

²² Return, O faithless sons, [says the Lord, and] I will heal your faithlessness. [And they answer] Behold, we come to You, for You are the Lord our God.

Jeremiah 3:22 (AMP)

At this point I realised I needed healing. I began praying the scripture and in answering my prayers, He turned me to the study of His Word and gradually enlightened my understanding. He showed me the key to faith. You cannot have faith without searching the scriptures, reading, studying, meditating and communicating the Word of God.

I discovered awesome things by the power of the Holy Spirit that culminated in the inspiration to write this book. The Word of God came alive to me and in me. I knew something different crept into my soul and I started believing the words I read. It began to make more sense to me, I enjoyed reading the scriptures, and one day during one of our church services, full clarity struck. The Pastor clarified that faith is a divine illumination, nothing mental or emotional, but divine. Faith comes when you get a revelation of the Word of God and this revelation changes your orientation and perception of life in the area in which you got the revelation.

Do not approach faith with the impossible mind set, but acknowledge you need to change your faith level and ask the Holy Spirit for help. The Holy Spirit is our comforter, advocate, teacher and helper. When you ask for faith, He will lead you through the path to achieving it. Learn to ask for help, that is why Jesus said *"whatsoever you ask my Father in my name He will give you"*.

All you can do is constantly apply yourself to His Word, and the light in the Word would lighten your understanding. It is how much you put into the word of God that will determine what you get out of it.

[38] *Now the just shall live by faith: but if any man draw back, my soul shall have no pleasure in him.*

Hebrews 10:38

If you desire to be just, you have to live and walk by faith and not by sight 2 *Corinthians 5:7*.

> ⁷ *(For we walk by faith, not by sight:)*
>
> *2 Corinthians 5:7*

Faith is the cure for unbelief. The Bible tells us to beware of an unbelieving heart.

> ¹² *[Therefore beware] brethren, take care, lest there be in any one of you a wicked, unbelieving heart [which refuses to cleave to, trust in, and rely on Him], leading you to turn away and desert or stand aloof from the living God.*
>
> *Hebrews 3:12 (AMP)*

Unbelief is equated with evil, so you cannot please God in unbelief. Unbelief on our part is saying that God is a liar and He will not answer any prayer that mocks His person. You must believe all that God has said concerning Himself and concerning you. As a seed of Abraham, a child of God, and a co-heir with Christ Jesus in all spiritual and heavenly blessings, you do need faith and must exercise yourself spiritually to get it.

The great Bible scholar, F. Dakes, in his works, identified 18 things that faith is. Faith is:

1. *The substance of things hoped for.*

2. *The evidence of things not seen.*

3. *The invincible backing of elders.*

4. *The creative power of divine works.*

5. *The divine testimony of right doing.*

6. *The cancellation of natural laws.*

7. *The basis for pleasing God.*

8.   *The dependence upon God's word.*

9.   *The ability to trust in an unknown future.*

10.   *The counting things that be not as thou they were.*

11.   *The ability to see invincible things.*

12.   *The assurance of God's faithfulness.*

13.   *The confidence in things to come,*

14.   *The stimulus of Christianity.*

15.   *The life blood of the just.*

16.   *The shield of Christian armour.*

17.   *The down payment of things desired.*

18.   *The guarantee of answered prayer.*

Your faith in God is what is counted for righteousness, for Abraham believed God and it was counted unto him for righteousness, so your faith is what justifies you.

> [2] *For if Abraham were justified by works, he hath whereof to glory; but not before God.*
> [3] *For what saith the scripture? Abraham believed God, and it was counted unto him for righteousness.*
> [4] *Now to him that worketh is the reward not reckoned of grace, but of debt.*
> [5] *But to him that worketh not, but believeth on him that justifieth the ungodly, his faith is counted for righteousness.*
>
> Romans 4:2-5

Faith gives you access into the grace of God where you stand and rejoice in hope of the glory of God to stand trials and tribulations without losing hope or giving up.

> [1] *Therefore being justified by faith, we have peace with God through our Lord Jesus Christ:*

² By whom also we have access by faith into this grace wherein we stand, and rejoice in hope of the glory of God.

³ And not only so, but we glory in tribulations also: knowing that tribulation worketh patience;

⁴ And patience, experience; and experience, hope:

⁵ And hope maketh not ashamed; because the love of God is shed abroad in our hearts by the Holy Ghost which is given unto us.

Romans 5:1-5

Remember it is through Abraham's faith that the whole world is saved and it is through faith that you are blessed in Abraham. Faith makes men sons and heirs in God's family rather than servants. Faith makes you a friend of God.

Getting unwavering faith

What steps do you need to take to get the spiritual information or wisdom that invokes unwavering faith?

¹⁷ So faith comes by hearing [what is told], and what is heard comes by the preaching [of the message that came from the lips] of Christ (the Messiah Himself).

Romans 10:17 (AMP)

¹⁷ So faith comes from hearing, that is, hearing the Good News about Christ.

Romans 10:17 (NLT)

From this scripture, we see that faith comes from hearing the Word of God. You cannot obtain faith outside of the Word of God. The key point is the Word of God. You need to hear the Word of God in your inner man. Notice it says "hearing". For you to hear, someone must be speaking. The spoken Word of God you hear comes from a variety of ways which include hearing directly from God, hearing through gifts (ministers) he has placed in the Church.

> ³ *And he humbled thee, and suffered thee to hunger, and fed thee with manna, which thou knewest not, neither did thy fathers know; that he might make thee know that man doth not live by bread only, but by every word that proceedeth out of the mouth of the LORD doth man live.*
>
> *Deuteronomy 8:3*

The word of God must be pursued and we have already established that the Word of God is Jesus Christ. To know Jesus, you must first own a Bible as it is the documented Word of God. It is meant to be searched out as your life depends on every word contained in it. You must come into the knowledge of the Son of God.

> ¹³ *Till we all come in the unity of the faith, and of the knowledge of the Son of God, unto a perfect man, unto the measure of the stature of the fulness of Christ:*
>
> *Ephesians 4:13*

The Word of God gives you knowledge about the Trinity and helps you understand how they operate. It is your relationship with the Word of God that brings faith. The Word of God opens you up to receive light that anchors you in the truth until you gradually become grounded in the truth of the Word. You must seek after the Lord and you will find Him. He is not far from you. Your heart must be ready and willing to receive the Word of God. You must have a sincere longing for His Word and you must search it out daily.

> ¹¹ *These were more noble than those in Thessalonica, in that they received the word with all readiness of mind, and searched the scriptures daily, whether those things were so.*
>
> *Acts 17:11*

It is in searching the Word of truth that you get built up and it gives you an inheritance among those who are sanctified (*Acts 20:32*).

Chapter Summary

Faith is the principle of inward and whole hearted confidence, assurance, trust and reliance on God and all that He says in His Word.

You cannot have faith without searching the scriptures, reading, studying, meditating and communicating the Word of God.

Chapter 8

Developing in your Identity I

*W*ithout knowledge of the Word of God, there is not much you can do as a believer. It is like having an *Aston Martin vantage V12* and not possess the keys to the car. It will always be yours but you will never have the luxury of enjoying the drive. The key to your successful walk with God is in your knowledge of the Word of God. *Deuteronomy 8:3* puts it in clear terms that man shall not live by bread alone but man lives by every word that proceeds from the mouth of God. Man was created to fulfil a purpose. This purpose can only be discovered by finding out from man's creator, what His original intention was.

In order to discover where you fit into in the master plan or purpose of God, there are a few spiritual exercises that can help you on this journey of discovery. Discovering identity is a function of how well you are able to exercise yourself in these areas.

Let us look at some of these simple concepts.

1. Studying the Word of God

If you want to grow, if you want to experience the glory of God in your life, you need to search the scriptures just as you eat food to grow and sustain your life. You need to know what God has said concerning the situation or circumstance before you. Without the word of God dwelling richly within you, you will not have the revelation that produces faith. The enemy does not recognise your opinion. He only recognises the revelation you possess in your heart.

> [15] *Study and be eager and do your utmost to present yourself to God approved (tested by trial), a workman who has no cause to be ashamed, correctly analyzing and accurately dividing [rightly handling and skillfully teaching] the Word of Truth.*
>
> 2 Timothy 2:15 (AMP)

The Word of God is the road that leads to the truth of God, and the truth leads to life. Studying the Word of God builds you up in faith. When the Bible says *'man shall not live by bread alone but by every word that proceeds from God'*, this means that your existence requires more than material things to be meaningful. You require the life giving, sustaining power of the word of God.

See the instruction God gave the children of Israel in *Isaiah 34:16* concerning their attitude to His Word. This is still relevant today.

> [16] *Seek ye out of the book of the LORD, and read: no one of these shall fail, none shall want her mate: for my mouth it hath commanded, and his spirit it hath gathered them.*
>
> Isaiah 34:16

A great injustice you can do to yourself is not to be acquainted with the Word of God. There is something quite interesting that I have noticed among believers, we read almost any other thing about God without reading the Bible. There are quite a number of study aids out there, christian books, tapes, CDs and many more that we could use as study aids but these things should be used in conjunction with our study of the Bible and not a replacement for Bible. The Bible should be your primary source of information and knowledge with study aids helping to provide further clarity.

Studying the Word of God needs to become a delight for you. Until you approach the Bible with a simple and trusting heart, you will never derive joy from reading it. If you do not have great anticipation to know God, the Bible will be a historical book that feeds your intellect without feeding your spirit. The study of the Word of God requires a thirst in your soul.

> [1] *As the hart panteth after the water brooks, so panteth my soul after thee, O God.*
> [2] *My soul thirsteth for God, for the living God: when shall I come and appear before God?*
>
> *Psalm 42:1-2*

When you thirst after God like David, the Bible becomes a sweet delight. God does not judge by the external appearance. He looks beyond the physical appearance and checks the state of the heart.

In the Bible you will get great and mighty revelations, you find words of comfort, admiration, words of encouragement from God to you. I remember the day I came across the scripture in *Zechariah 1:14*

> [14] *So the angel that communed with me said unto me, Cry thou, saying, Thus saith the LORD of hosts; I am jealous for Jerusalem and for Zion with a great jealousy.*
>
> *Zechariah 1:14*

This gave me a tingle in my tummy and I was excited because I had just discovered by revelation a dimension of what God thinks about me. There are so many things to discover in the Word of truth, yet it is the last thing many believers want to read.

Studying the Word of God gives revelation that transforms you into a fearless, authority holding, dominion exercising firebrand believer. It is the vehicle through which the will of God is discovered and arrows of light from heaven are released to you. It is when you fortify your heart with the word that it becomes impossible for the enemy to deceive you and mislead you.

The Word of God is likened to wisdom in *Proverbs 2:6*

> *⁶ For the LORD giveth wisdom: out of his mouth cometh knowledge and understanding.*

> *Proverbs 2:6*

We are advised to hold wisdom in high esteem. When you embrace wisdom it will bring promotion and honour.

> *⁷ Wisdom is the principal thing; therefore get wisdom: and with all thy getting get understanding.*
> *⁸ Exalt her, and she shall promote thee: she shall bring thee to honour, when thou dost embrace her.*

> *Proverbs 4:7-8*

The entire book of Proverbs talks about godly wisdom, what it is and its effect in the life of a believer. The wisdom that is spoken about here is the Word of God, the instructions of God telling us how to live life and helping us make the right choices in life. It gives you insight on what is profitable and what is not. Wisdom is more precious than rubies, it is the tree of life to those who find it.

> *¹⁸ She is a tree of life to them that lay hold upon her: and happy is*

every one that retaineth her.

Proverbs 3:18

Wisdom is Jesus Christ, He is the power and the wisdom of God. Jesus is God's speech in living form, He is the wisdom spoken by God that created all things

> ²⁴ *But unto them which are called, both Jews and Greeks, Christ the power of God, and the wisdom of God.*

1 Corinthians 1:24

We must do everything to study the Bible which will lead us to wisdom (Jesus). To seek after the knowledge of God with devotion is the beginning of wisdom. The Bible is the inspired word of God.

2. *Understanding the Word of God*

Getting understanding is a very critical component of understanding your identity. It is possible for you to read and study a subject without getting to the point of understanding. When studying the Bible, we notice that we are instructed to get understanding.

> ⁷ *Wisdom is the principal thing; therefore get wisdom: and with all thy getting get understanding.*
> ⁸ *Exalt her, and she shall promote thee: she shall bring thee to honour, when thou dost embrace her.*

Proverbs 4:7-8

Understanding, in this context, is getting revelation of the truth in the word of God. It is getting to the point when you know why something is done in a particular way. You come to a point where you know the knowledge behind the action. Understanding is like a light that brightens your spirit man, it is enlightenment for your own spirit. With understanding, you do not only realise what was done, you also know why it was done the way it was done. Having understanding is crucial because without understanding, you take things out of context. See Paul's prayer for the Ephesians.

> [17] [For I always pray to] the God of our Lord Jesus Christ, the Father of glory, that He may grant you a spirit of wisdom and revelation [of insight into mysteries and secrets] in the [deep and intimate] knowledge of Him,
> [18] By having the eyes of your heart flooded with light, so that you can know and understand the hope to which He has called you, and how rich is His glorious inheritance in the saints (His set-apart ones),
>
> *Ephesians 1:17-18 (AMP)*

Enlightenment brings about clear knowledge of God, giving you insight. It is the Holy Spirit that brings illumination. So what *Proverbs 4:7-8* is simply saying is get Jesus and in getting Jesus get the Holy Spirit, the Spirit of Christ that will reveal all things to you. Receiving true understanding goes beyond human intelligence. If you look at the lives of the Pharisees and Sadducees, they were the law keepers and teachers, yet the Messiah they were earnestly seeking and waiting for was in their midst and they could not discern Him. Familiarity with the Bible will not give you spiritual understanding if all you do is read the Bible as an intellectual or mental exercise. It may tickle your senses like any other book of stories would, but until the Holy Spirit pours out revelation knowledge, the Bible will only remain a book of many interesting stories.

The key to getting spiritual understanding or revelation knowledge is to approach the study of the Bible with an expectant heart that you would learn something new and that the Holy Spirit will shine light on the Word to give you a deeper understanding. When you get this understanding and revelation knowledge of God, your life will never be the same like Saul who saw the light and heard the voice of God on his way to Damascus in an experience that brought a transformation. It marked the end of Saul and the beginning of Paul the Apostle of Christ. This understanding I am talking about is a personal thing. When Saul saw the light and heard the voice, the voice pierced his heart and broke away the hardness. While everyone around him saw the light but only Saul heard the voice. I believe many are seeing the light today but not hearing the voice. It takes hearing the voice for understanding to come.

Your love for the Word of God must push you to seek revelation knowledge from God everyday of your life. This is your daily bread. Solomon in *Proverbs 21:16* advices us;

> [16] *The man that wandereth out of the way of understanding shall remain in the congregation of the dead.*

Proverbs 21:16

Understanding brings you into the company of the living, that is the company of the blessed. Make a decision today to apply yourself diligently to the study of the word of God and pray that as you take up your Bible, the Holy Spirit will illuminate your mind and draw you closer to God. The aim of it all is to get to know God better and build a relationship with Him. I believe that as you do that, you will definitely see a change in your life.

3. *Meditating on the Word of God*

A simple definition of Meditation is; *a continuous contemplation or reflective thought on a subject or series of subjects.* Meditation is to reflect deeply, chew over, think intently by keeping the mind fixed on a subject, with a view to gaining understanding. In Christian circles, It is having mind conversations using the Word of God.

When you meditate on the Word of God, you are fixing your mind on the things that you have read, constantly running over the Word in your mind. Meditation is something God commands us to do. If God Himself recommends meditation, then it must be important for the believer.

> [8] *This book of the law shall not depart out of thy mouth; but thou shalt meditate therein day and night, that thou mayest observe to do according to all that is written therein: for then thou shalt make thy way prosperous, and then thou shalt have good success.*
>
> *Joshua 1:8*

Meditation gives you a deep sense of what the word is talking about and opens you up to more clarity in the Word of God. *Psalms 1:2*, like *Joshua 1:8* instructs us to meditate on the Law of God day and night.

> [2] *But his delight is in the law of the LORD; and in his law doth he meditate day and night.*
>
> *Psalm 1:2*

There is something similar in both quoted scriptures which is *"meditating on the Word of God day and night"*. The key point *"day and night"* is referring to consistency. It therefore means that the word of God should constantly be in your thoughts. It means to be filled with imaginations of the Word of God. This process helps to build up the much-needed faith because you constantly have your mind fixed on God and His Word. Meditation is the process of getting the Word firmly implanted and rooted in your heart.

> [21] *Wherefore lay apart all filthiness and superfluity of naughtiness, and receive with meekness the engrafted word, which is able to save your souls.*
>
> *James 1:21*

Meditation is the gate to gaining wisdom, knowledge and insight regarding the things of God. The more of His Word you get to know the more you build up your spiritual life and relationship with God. Meditation brings you closer to the heart of God. Meditation demonstrates you are trying to understand the workings of God's mind as you ponder on the things He said. One of the reasons God spoke so highly of king David as the man after His own heart is because David sought to understand the mind of God and the things that moved God. Look at some of the things David said concerning meditation

> *⁶ When I remember thee upon my bed, and meditate on thee in the night watches.*
> *⁷ Because thou hast been my help, therefore in the shadow of thy wings will I rejoice.*
>
> *Psalm 63:6-7*

> *¹² I will meditate also of all thy work, and talk of thy doings.*
>
> *Psalm 77:12*

> *⁹⁷ O how love I thy law! it is my meditation all the day.*
> *⁹⁸ Thou through thy commandments hast made me wiser than mine enemies: for they are ever with me.*
> *⁹⁹ I have more understanding than all my teachers: for thy testimonies are my meditation.*
>
> *Psalm 119:97-99*

Through David's meditation, he learnt to respect the ways of God (*Psalm 119:15*), he learnt to be glad in the Lord and found sweetness in it (*Psalms 104:34*).

In the New Testament, we see another similar instruction on meditation, just in case you are thinking meditation passed away in the Old Testament. Apostle Paul instructed Timothy to meditate.

> *¹⁴ Neglect not the gift that is in thee, which was given thee by prophecy, with the laying on of the hands of the presbytery.*
> *¹⁵ Meditate upon these things; give thyself wholly to them; that thy profiting may appear to all.*
>
> *1 Timothy 4:14-15*

There is immense profit in meditation. In meditating on the things concerning God, you revive areas of the mind that were not functioning. It is the path that leads you to good success and make you become the envy of others. It brings forth material prosperity and gives you the opportunity to walk in the perfect will of God for your life. Meditation is like writing the word of God on the tables of your heart so it becomes unforgettable. One of the keys to meditation is *day and night,* that is, dedication and consistency. Familiarise yourself with this practice, develop your friendship with the Word of God and apply the knowledge gained as the guide in your daily life. The wisdom you attain from studying and meditating on the Word of God sets you apart from the rest.

> [6] *Howbeit we speak wisdom among them that are perfect: yet not the wisdom of this world, nor of the princes of this world, that come to nought:*
> [7] *But we speak the wisdom of God in a mystery, even the hidden wisdom, which God ordained before the world unto our glory:*
>
> *1 Corinthians 2:6-7*

Paul explains to the people at Corinth that *"yet when we are among the full grown spiritually mature Christians who are ripe in understanding, we do impart a higher wisdom the knowledge of the divine plan previously hidden; but it is indeed not a wisdom for this present age... ".*

> [4] *[The [Servant of God says] The Lord God has given Me the tongue of a disciple and of one who is taught, that I should know how to speak a word in season to him who is weary. He wakens Me morning by morning, He wakens My ear to hear as a disciple [as one who is taught].*
>
> *Isaiah 50:4 (AMP)*

4. Communicating the Word.

This exercise is one a lot of believers usually stumble on.

This is when you verbalise your study and meditations into words that can be communicated to others. Look at *Joshua 1:8* again.

> ⁸ *This book of the law shall not depart out of thy mouth; but thou shalt meditate therein day and night, that thou mayest observe to do according to all that is written therein: for then thou shalt make thy way prosperous, and then thou shalt have good success.*

Joshua 1:8

It says *"this book of the law shall not depart out of thy mouth..."* When you study and meditate on the word, it is worthwhile to communicate the word or simply put, profess the word. Speaking the Word of God out of your mouth means you hear yourself. *Psalm 107:2* says *"let the redeemed of the Lord say so, whom He hath redeemed from the hand of the enemy."* The point in this scripture is that the redeemed of the Lord should say so. The deliverance is in the saying. The word is not meant to remain in you. You are expected to apply the word to situations, and the way to do this application is by speaking the Word of God.

Communicating the Word of God is done in various ways; through prayer, exhortation, witnessing, preaching and teaching and declarations. In *Ephesians 5:19*, Paul instructs the believers in Ephesus to *speak to themselves in Psalms and hymns and in spiritual songs, singing and making melody in their hearts to the Lord. 1 Peter 4:11* tells us to *speak as oracles of God*, meaning you should speak as though God Himself were speaking through you. How does God speak? He spoke and speaks the very words that you read and meditate on in the Bible. I use the word *speaks* because His words are life and still exist and will continue to exist and be alive. Speak the Word of God until it becomes part of you. *John 3:34* states that *"he who God sends speaks the words of God"*. In all that you do, your speech should reflect God and glorify His name.

Paul in *Colossians 3:16* says that *"the word of Christ dwell in you richly in all wisdom; teaching and admonishing one another is Psalms and hymns and spiritual songs, singing with grace in your hearts to the Lord"*. Your speech is required to be holy, wise, courteous, respectful, desirable, gracious, savoury, wholesome, that is worthy to be kept in the memory of others. Words that glorify God, not corrupt, vain, offensive, perverse, carnal, crude, vulgar, or rude words (*Colossians 4:6*). Your words should be words that oppose sin. Protect your words from corruption, let your words be words that build.

Speak God's word to open and close the spirit realm, for God has given you the authority to do so, (*Matthew 18:19*), Jesus said that He has given the keys to the kingdom of Heaven: whatsoever we bind on earth is bound in Heaven, and whatsoever we loose on earth shall be loose in Heaven. Heaven exists in the spirit realm that we cannot see but we have the keys to operate there. *Matthew 18:18* restates the same thing, you do not bind anything in the spirit realm physically but through your words. The spirit realm is where it matters most, it is the realm that determines what goes on in the physical realm. It will be wise to get a good understanding of what goes on in the spirit realm and how to work the spirit realm with our words.

Spoken words are carriers of miraculous power. The power of the spoken Word of God was taught by Jesus to His disciples.

> [20] *He said to them, Because of the littleness of your faith [that is, your lack of [firmly relying trust]. For truly I say to you, if you have faith [that is living] like a grain of mustard seed, you can say to this mountain, Move from here to yonder place, and it will move; and*

nothing will be impossible to you.

Matthew 17:20 (AMP)

You have to speak the Word of God to activate the power behind it. *Romans 4:17* says that *God called the things that are not as though they were.* You are to call the things that are not as though they are in your life. Your victory in life is based on the knowledge of God you have and the degree to which you use them in utterances and decrees. When there are things going contrary to the promises of God in your life, you can counter these things by making prophetic utterances based on the Word of God. Learn to declare, command and establish the Word of God in your life. Remember Jesus said in *Mark 9:23* that if you can believe, all things are possible to you. You can only speak the things you believe. As you make these decrees your faith is built up. Great miracles have been wrought by speaking the Word of God only. Let us look at two of them.

Sun and Moon stand still at the Spoken Word

Looking at the this account, Joshua spoke to the sun and the moon to stand still that he may fight the battle and establish God's will, and the sun and moon obeyed. It is recorded that God harkened to the voice of Joshua and fought for Israel.

¹² Then spake Joshua to the LORD in the day when the LORD delivered up the Amorites before the children of Israel, and he said in the sight of Israel, Sun, stand thou still upon Gibeon; and thou, Moon, in the valley of Ajalon.
¹³ And the sun stood still, and the moon stayed, until the people had avenged themselves upon their enemies. Is not this written in the book of Jasher? So the sun stood still in the midst of heaven, and hasted not to go down about a whole day.
¹⁴ And there was no day like that before it or after it, that the LORD

hearkened unto the voice of a man: for the LORD fought for Israel.

Joshua 10:12-14

Water comes out of a rock at the Spoken Word

God instructed Moses to gather the people of Israel and speak to the rock before the children of Israel and water would come forth out of the rock. God's power is activated through words, so get into the programme of speaking the word, prophesying the word, witnessing the word, because the angels in heaven are waiting for you to speak His word so they can execute it speedily.

[7] And the LORD spake unto Moses, saying,
[8] Take the rod, and gather thou the assembly together, thou, and Aaron thy brother, and speak ye unto the rock before their eyes; and it shall give forth his water, and thou shalt bring forth to them water out of the rock: so thou shalt give the congregation and their beasts drink.

Numbers 20:7-8

Proclaim the Word of God when it is convenient and when it is not, encourage, inspire, give hope and counsel with the Word of God. Give earnest advice, help others to be free from confusion through words of edification, help others gain spiritual improvement, advocate, remind one another of the Word of God in the Bible. Search the scriptures deeply. Be careful not to distort or misinterpret it to fit what you think.

The Word of God has to find its expression in your heart before you can truly bear fruit.

[4] Abide in me, and I in you. As the branch cannot bear fruit of itself, except it abide in the vine; no more can ye, except ye abide in me.
[5] I am the vine, ye are the branches: He that abideth in me, and I in him, the same bringeth forth much fruit: for without me ye can do

nothing

John 15:4-5

Speaking the word without ceasing infuses the word into your heart. You must become like David who was so much in love with God that he proclaimed in *Psalms 119:103 that the words of God are sweet to taste, sweeter than honey in his mouth.*

Chapter Summary

The key to your successful walk with God is in your knowledge in the Word of God.

The Bible should be your primary source of information and knowledge with study aids helping to provide further clarity.

You have to speak the Word of God to activate the power behind it.

Chapter 9

Developing in your Identity II

*A*nother important aspect of developing your identity that is a catalyst for great things *is having respect for Prayer*. Prayer is nothing elaborate, complicated or boring. I cannot believe I could ever make this kind of assertion in this lifetime. Phew! Did I abhor prayer growing up! Prayer time for me was a time of punishment. If you wanted to make me miserable, all you needed to do was call a prayer time. I disliked night vigils except it had to do with lots of singing. Anything that incorporated long hours of praying was just not my turf. I just could not understand why we had to be gathered in a place with a prayer point list summing up to a hundred. All my mind could think of at that point was when would they pray the last point so I could go home.

At these meetings, you would find some people screaming, some jumping and some weeping. I found it quite amusing and would go home and mimic these people. This formed a very wrong notion and mindset for me. I was very disinterested in prayer. I loved praise and worship but not prayer. I just could not understand what was being said for hours unending. Oh my! I was very wrong and I thank God for His wonderful Spirit that teaches and clarifies things.

In simple terms, prayer means talking to or speaking with God. It is an act of communicating with God where reverent petitions are made and *Kingdom business* is discussed. It is not a monologue where the only person speaking is you. Prayer is a dialogue where you talk with God and He talks with you. All prayer is not the same. There are different forms of prayer. There is t*he prayer of supplication, prayer of intercession, prayer of agreement, prayer of dedication or consecration, thanksgiving, praise and worship.*

Prayer of Supplication

Prayer of Supplication is a heart earnestly crying out to God concerning a need. It is acknowledging that God is your source and He is the one who supplies all of your needs. It is appealing or entreating God for some need. It is not coming to Him as a backup plan after all else has failed but knowing in your core that it is only God that can do it for you. It is beseeching Him until you get what you are asking for. It is a strong incessant pleading.

> [1] *I exhort therefore, that, first of all, supplications, prayers, intercessions, and giving of thanks, be made for all men;*
> [2] *For kings, and for all that are in authority; that we may lead a quiet and peaceable life in all godliness and honesty.*
>
> 1 Timothy 2:1-2

When the word *supplication* comes up in the Bible, it is usually used in the context of prayer. Paul used the word again when writing to the Philippians.

⁶ Be careful for nothing; but in every thing by prayer and supplication with thanksgiving let your requests be made known unto God.

Philippians 4:6

We are encouraged to tell God all of our needs, be it material, physical or spiritual needs. Anything that has to do with our lives must be put in prayer before God. Supplication requires persistence and perseverance. The great prophet of God Elijah was one given to this kind of prayer. He earnestly prayed for the rains to cease and they ceased. He prayed for the rains to start again and they did.

¹⁷ Elias was a man subject to like passions as we are, and he prayed earnestly that it might not rain: and it rained not on the earth by the space of three years and six months.
¹⁸ And he prayed again, and the heaven gave rain, and the earth brought forth her fruit.

James 5:17-18

This example illustrates how powerful prayer is when it is done with an assurance that it will be answered. All prayer requires of you is to believe in the God you are praying to.

²² And all things, whatsoever ye shall ask in prayer, believing, ye shall receive.

Matthew 21:22

Jesus in *Luke 18:1* advices us to always pray and not faint, not to give in to doubt, fear, unbelief, discouragement or give up when prayer seems unanswered. Rebuke and resist everything contrary suggestion of failure to your prayer. It is a divine blood bought right to have your prayers answered. Jesus has paid the price for our prayers to be answered. Do not lose heart, Jesus has promised that as long as you ask, just simply believe that you have received it. More often than not, this will go against your senses. The situation may look impossible but remember, God is greater than your mind.

Prayer of Intercession

Prayer of intercession is pleading the cause of another person. There are numerous examples in the Bible of people who interceded on behalf of others.

Abraham interceded for Sodom and Gomorrah.

> *23 And Abraham drew near, and said, Wilt thou also destroy the righteous with the wicked?*
> *24 Peradventure there be fifty righteous within the city: wilt thou also destroy and not spare the place for the fifty righteous that are therein?*
> *25 That be far from thee to do after this manner, to slay the righteous with the wicked: and that the righteous should be as the wicked, that be far from thee: Shall not the Judge of all the earth do right?*
> *26 And the LORD said, If I find in Sodom fifty righteous within the city, then I will spare all the place for their sakes.*
> *27 And Abraham answered and said, Behold now, I have taken upon me to speak unto the LORD, which am but dust and ashes:*
> *28 Peradventure there shall lack five of the fifty righteous: wilt thou destroy all the city for lack of five? And he said, If I find there forty and five, I will not destroy it.*
> *29 And he spake unto him yet again, and said, Peradventure there shall be forty found there. And he said, I will not do it for forty's sake.*
> *30 And he said unto him, Oh let not the LORD be angry, and I will speak: Peradventure there shall thirty be found there. And he said, I will not do it, if I find thirty there.*
> *31 And he said, Behold now, I have taken upon me to speak unto the LORD: Peradventure there shall be twenty found there. And he said, I will not destroy it for twenty's sake.*
> *32 And he said, Oh let not the LORD be angry, and I will speak yet but this once: Peradventure ten shall be found there. And he said, I will not destroy it for ten's sake.*
> *33 And the LORD went his way, as soon as he had left communing with Abraham: and Abraham returned unto his place.*

Genesis 18:23-33

Elisha interceded for the dead son of the Shunammite woman.

> [32] And when Elisha was come into the house, behold, the child was dead, and laid upon his bed.
> [33] He went in therefore, and shut the door upon them twain, and prayed unto the LORD.
> [34] And he went up, and lay upon the child, and put his mouth upon his mouth, and his eyes upon his eyes, and his hands upon his hands: and stretched himself upon the child; and the flesh of the child waxed warm.
> [35] Then he returned, and walked in the house to and fro; and went up, and stretched himself upon him: and the child sneezed seven times, and the child opened his eyes.
> [36] And he called Gehazi, and said, Call this Shunammite. So he called her. And when she was come in unto him, he said, Take up thy son.

2 Kings 4:32-36

The early Church interceded for Peter.

> [5] Peter therefore was kept in prison: but prayer was made without ceasing of the church unto God for him.

Acts 12:5

Intercession is very important; it shifts the focus off you and allows you to think about others. It breaks away the wall of selfishness in our lives. God loves intercessors because their hearts are endeared towards other people. They want to see the will of God take place in the lives of other people. Intercession makes you people conscious and ignites the spirit of benevolence.

Prayer of Agreement

The prayer of agreement is the prayer of two or more people coming together to agree on a common goal. This is a very powerful type of prayer because it is two spirits joining their faith together and it brings about tremendous results.

> ¹⁹ *Again I say unto you, That if two of you shall agree on earth as touching any thing that they shall ask, it shall be done for them of my Father which is in heaven.*
> ²⁰ *For where two or three are gathered together in my name, there am I in the midst of them.*

Matthew 18:19-20

The church ought to use the prayer of agreement to establish the will of God here on earth, to overcome obstacles and break barriers and possess territories. It is also a weapon that couples and families should engage in more often than not to keep the family united and resist the fiery darts of the enemy.

> ⁸ *There is one alone, and there is not a second; yea, he hath neither child nor brother: yet is there no end of all his labour; neither is his eye satisfied with riches; neither saith he, For whom do I labour, and bereave my soul of good? This is also vanity, yea, it is a sore travail.*
> ⁹ *Two are better than one; because they have a good reward for their labour.*
> ¹⁰ *For if they fall, the one will lift up his fellow: but woe to him that is alone when he falleth; for he hath not another to help him up.*
> ¹¹ *Again, if two lie together, then they have heat: but how can one be warm alone?*
> ¹² *And if one prevail against him, two shall withstand him; and a threefold cord is not quickly broken.*

Ecclesiastes 4:8-12

Ecclesiastes 4:8-12 lays the principle that a threefold cord is not easily broken, if one person is prevailed against the other two shall stand with him. I believe one of the reasons we see the family institution, the marriage institution and the church not achieving their full potential today is that there is no genuine unity or should I say togetherness. Husband and wife do not pray together as they should, we do not pray together in church or agree on anything as we should. We do not even pray for each other as we should because we are so consumed by our own needs that we can barely think of the next person to the point of even praying for them. What we have failed to understand is the fact that our relationship with God especially in the place of prayer determines our relationship with one another.

Prayer of Consecration or Dedication

When you are in need of strength to accomplish the will of God, venturing into ministry, unknown territories in the work of God, the prayer of consecration or dedication is important. It is a prayer to God, humbly submitting to His will. Jesus in His hour of crucifixion prayed this prayer type of prayer.

> [39] *And he came out, and went, as he was wont, to the mount of Olives; and his disciples also followed him.*
> [40] *And when he was at the place, he said unto them, Pray that ye enter not into temptation.*
> [41] *And he was withdrawn from them about a stone's cast, and kneeled down, and prayed,*
> [42] *Saying, Father, if thou be willing, remove this cup from me: nevertheless not my will, but thine, be done.*
> [43] *And there appeared an angel unto him from heaven, strengthening him.*
> [44] *And being in an agony he prayed more earnestly: and his sweat was as it were great drops of blood falling down to the ground.*
>
> *Luke 22:39-44*

The burden Jesus felt was overwhelming. We read in *verse 44* that He was in agony but went to God in prayer seeking strength and help, in the hour of horrid darkness, to carry Him through the plans He came to earth for. So do not imagine that you can walk the walk of ministry without going to God for strength. In *Romans 12:1*, we are told to present our bodies as a living sacrifice, holy and acceptable unto God which is our reasonable service. Consecration is setting yourself apart for God to do His will, to sanctify yourself, making yourself a temple worthy for the Holy Spirit of God to dwell in and a vessel that is worthy to be used for good works.

Prayer of Faith

All forms of prayer are anchored on faith. In the prayer of faith, your full trust is firmly fixed on the word of God. You cannot pray right if you do not know the word of God. The prayer of faith is a prayer you pray once concerning the issue at hand. Praying the prayer of faith more than once on an issue represents unbelief.

> [22] *And Jesus answering saith unto them, Have faith in God.*
> [23] *For verily I say unto you, That whosoever shall say unto this mountain, Be thou removed, and be thou cast into the sea; and shall not doubt in his heart, but shall believe that those things which he saith shall come to pass; he shall have whatsoever he saith.*
> [24] *Therefore I say unto you, What things soever ye desire, when ye pray, believe that ye receive them, and ye shall have them.*
>
> *Mark 11:22-24*

Praying in the Spirit or Praying in tongues

Praying in the Spirit or Praying in tongues is also important. When you pray in tongues you are praying to God and you speak mysteries. Praying in tongues edifies you as we earlier discovered, you speak the language no man understands except God and it is inspired by the Holy Spirit. When you pray in tongues, you do not know what you speak nor have an understanding of what your are praying for. That is why it is called speaking mysteries.

> [14] *For if I pray in an unknown tongue, my spirit prayeth, but my*

understanding is unfruitful.

15 *What is it then? I will pray with the spirit, and I will pray with the understanding also: I will sing with the spirit, and I will sing with the understanding also.*

1 Corinthians 14:14-15

The Holy Spirit knows exactly what you are praying about and sometimes gives you interpretation. Praying in tongues is a great personal blessing for a believer.

Thanksgiving

Thanksgiving is acknowledging the things that God is doing or has done or will do in your life. It is acknowledging God as your source keeping you grounded and away from pride. Thanksgiving is acknowledging that you would not be where you are or achieve anything in this life except for the grace and mercies of God. You are grounded from getting all puffed up with lofty ideas that you forget where you are coming from.

18 *In every thing give thanks: for this is the will of God in Christ Jesus concerning you.*

1 Thessalonians 5:18

We are instructed to enter God's presence with thanksgiving and praise, and to be thankful to Him and bless His name *Psalm 100:4. Psalm 95:2* reiterates the same thing. Come before the Lord with thanksgiving. Thanksgiving is essential prayer you need to enter into His presence to make your petition known. Your attitude therefore should be an attitude of rejoicing that you are coming before a good God who is willing to hear and answer your petition.

Praise and Worship

Praise and worship is the fastest gateway into God's presence. There are many scriptures on praise. One man in the Bible we see that understood *Praise* was David the king. He could captivate God with his praise and bring delight to the heart of God. No wonder God referred to him as the man after His heart.

> ²² *And when he had removed him, he raised up unto them David to be their king; to whom also he gave their testimony, and said, I have found David the son of Jesse, a man after mine own heart, which shall fulfil all my will.*

> *Acts 13:22*

Praise touches the heart of God. It is offering grateful reverence to God in words or in song. Glorifying God and honouring God with all enthusiasm as an act of worship. *Psalm 22:3* says God is enthroned by our praises. It is expressing the greatness of God and all His works, expressing His infinite knowledge and great power, rejoicing in His word. *Psalms 100:2* says we should enter His presence with singing, He requires for us to be joyful in His presence, because *"in His presence there is fullness of joy and at His right there are pleasures forever more"* Almost the entire book of Psalms talks about praise and we can learn a lot about how to praise and worship the only living God from that book of the Bible.

To buttress the importance of praise, Jesus in *Luke 19:40* responding to the Pharisees on His triumphant entry into Jerusalem, said to them that if He ordered the crowd to cease from praising Him, the stones would immediately cry out in praise to Him. So let everything that has breath praise the Lord. Resound His praises, exalt His name forever, and rejoice greatly in Jesus.

Worship is expressing our love to God in return for His love. Worship is our response to God's faithfulness and giving all of ourselves to Him in return. Worship is our bond with God, adoring, respecting, honouring, esteeming Him unconditionally. Worship is drawing close to God in a respectful and humble manner. It is focusing on who God is, waiting on God, knowing He wants to fellowship with you. Worship should be a consistent part of our daily exercise as believers. It should be one of the daily spiritual vitamins for our spirit man. God is looking for those who will worship Him in spirit and in truth.

> [24] *God is a Spirit: and they that worship him must worship him in spirit and in truth.*
>
> *John 4:24*

Our worship must be from a sincere heart, remember that He knows the contents of your heart, because He searches it *Jeremiah 17:10*. All that we are and have should be devoted to God. Worship is not about the songs you sing but what you truly feel in your heart. It is resounding your commitment to God. Worship is the life you live. It is what you were created for. *John 9:31b* says that *"God listens to those who worship Him"*.

Thanksgiving, praise and worship are very powerful weapons every believer needs. It disarms attacks from the devil and it helps to build up faith. There is a popular saying *that prayer moves the hands of God but praise moves God*. Even when times are rough and you enter into a phase of thanksgiving, you are simply telling God by your actions that you trust in Him not just in the good times but in the bad. Such praise is sweet incense to God. It should not be a ritual but reflections of a genuine commitment to God based on faithfulness to the relationship, desiring His presence more than anything else.

God does not like to be ignored and I am certain neither do you. He does not like to be taken for granted. You know how it feels like when the person or people you love so much do not acknowledge you or take you for granted. God thirsts for us to love Him back, He created us so that He could fellowship with us and build a relationship and a strong bond with us. He wants to share His mind and ideas with us as a friend to a friend. He needs us to reach out to Him as He reaches out to us. It hurts Him really bad that we do not love Him or care about Him. God has a heart and it aches too.

> ⁵ *Thus says the Lord: What unrighteousness did your fathers find in Me, that they went far from Me and [habitually] went after emptiness, falseness, and futility and themselves became fruitless and worthless?*
>
> *Jeremiah 2:5*

His feelings towards us again is seen in *Hosea 11:8*. He did not withhold His Son from the cross for us just so He could relate with us as a father to a child, friend to a friend. Is that not awesome? He does not joke with those who truly love Him and is truly excited with such people *1 Corinthians 2:8-9*. We need to make Him the most important person in our lives and consider Him first just as He puts us first like David did.

> ¹⁰ *And David enquired of God, saying, Shall I go up against the Philistines? And wilt thou deliver them into mine hand? And the LORD said unto him, Go up; for I will deliver them into thine hand.*
>
> *1 Chronicles 14:10*

David enquired from God if he should go to battle, and He gave David His go ahead. That is kind of relationship He desires of us.

Roadblocks to Prayer

Prayer is not gravelling or begging, prayer is not moaning, grumbling or weeping. I believe one reason we have so many unanswered prayers is due to the fact that we do not believe in our hearts that God can do what we are asking. We put reasoning, emotions and our circumstances above the word of God. There are a number of things that could impede answers to our prayers. Unbelief is a major prayer stopper. Self centred prayers are another obstacle. When in the place of prayer, we need to consider others and not just our own needs. Prayer is also hindered when it is not based on the Word of God. Prayer should be scriptural, purposeful and precise. We need to take God's words to Him in prayer as He cannot deal with us outside His Word. Scriptures can never be broken, for anything the Lord has spoken will come to pass.

> ²⁵ *For I am the LORD: I will speak, and the word that I shall speak shall come to pass; it shall be no more prolonged: for in your days, O rebellious house, will I say the word, and will perform it, saith the Lord GOD.*
>
> *Ezekiel 12:25*

If you need healing, search the Bible for scriptures on healing and what it says and pray the scripture basing your faith on the fact that He will perform all that He has spoken. Hold God to His words. He will never deny anything He has said or promised.

> ¹¹ *Thus saith the LORD, the Holy One of Israel, and his Maker, Ask me of things to come concerning my sons, and concerning the work of my hands command ye me.*
>
> *Isaiah 45:11*

It is established now that you are His son or daughter, He has given you the right to command Him, but it must be based on His word. What the Lord is saying to you here is this; *you should have so much faith in Him as to direct Him to fulfil your needs.* Imagine the fact that the creator of Heaven and earth, the seen and unseen, the One who formed and fashioned you and I, that can take the breath of life in a moment, says you should command Him.

To achieve anything as a believer living in victory, prayer is inevitable. Understand that you cannot do anything on your own. To get the empowerment to break barriers and to rise above all things, you must always be in the place of prayer. A praying believer who is grounded in the Word of God is a most dangerous weapon in God's hands. *WORD x Holy Spirit + PRAYER = A VICTORIOUS BELIEVER.* If there is anything missing in this equation, you will keep struggling. The Word of God brings empowerment and prayer releases the power.

We often suffer setbacks in life because we fail to exercise our right to pray. There is a very popular song which says *"what a friend we have in Jesus, all our sins and grief to bear, what a privilege to carry, everything to God in prayer, oh what peace we often forfeit oh what needless pains we bear, all because we do not carry, everything to God in prayer"*. We bear things we have no business bearing when the Lord has asked us to cast all of our cares upon Him for He cares for us *1 Peter 5:7. Psalms 55:22* declares that He will sustain you and He will never let the righteous to be moved.

When you are persistent in the place of prayer, you have the treasures of Heaven open to you. As long as you seek earnestly and desire the powers of Heaven to be made manifest here on earth, you have to pray. It is in the place of prayer that you get ministered to, just like Jesus, after forty days of prayer and fasting in *Matthew 4:11.*

We see again the efficacy of prayer in *Matthew 26:53* where Jesus talking to those who were to take Him captive *"thinkest thou that I cannot now pray to My Father, and He shall presently give me more than twelve legions of angels."*

So when you need help, you call on God in prayer. Prayer is the only channel through which Heaven can intervene in earthly matters. Earth is not God's jurisdiction and therefore He cannot step into matters here without being invited. Heaven can only intervene when you ask or call on God for help. Never give up. Tarry till you see results in that which you desire. The place of prayer is where you discover your true identity in Christ.

Chapter Summary

All prayer is not the same. There are different forms of prayer.

All forms of prayer are anchored on faith. In the prayer of faith, your full trust is firmly fixed on the word of God.

When you are persistent in the place of prayer, you have the treasures of Heaven open to you.

Chapter 10

I Am What I Think

For as he thinketh in his heart, so is he.

Proverb 23:7

*H*ow interesting the way the Bible sums up a man by the things he thinks about. Jesus buttresses the above statement in *Matthew 12:34* and made it clear that *"out of the abundance of the heart (the sum total of your thoughts) the mouth speaks"*. This means that what we hear people speak about is what they have been thinking about. Your mind is where thinking, reasoning and applying knowledge takes place. What you focus on sums up what you think. You should understand that if you feed your mind with garbage, you will in turn speak garbage. I am sure you are familiar with the slogan *garbage in garbage out*.

What things do you feed your mind with? What are your predominant thoughts? Those are the things that will ultimately shape who you will become.

Invariably the heart is either good or evil; the Bible does

not state anything in between.

> *34 O generation of vipers, how can ye, being evil, speak good things?*
> *for out of the abundance of the heart the mouth speaketh.*
> *35 A good man out of the good treasure of the heart bringeth forth*
> *good things: and an evil man out of the evil treasure bringeth forth*
> *evil things.*

Matthew 12:34-35

This is one of the reasons we are instructed to study the Word of God and meditate on it day and night. It is the meditating of the Word of God that shapes your mindset. You no longer think like those of the world and act like them because your mind is renewed and transformed.

> *22 That ye put off concerning the former conversation the old man,*
> *which is corrupt according to the deceitful lusts;*
> *23 And be renewed in the spirit of your mind;*
> *24 And that ye put on the new man, which after God is created in*
> *righteousness and true holiness.*

Ephesians 4:22-24

Your life should be directed towards God. You must manifest the nature of Christ in righteousness and holiness. It is very interesting to note that there are loads of believers who have said the *Prayer of salvation,* but have not had their minds renewed. They still retain their old thinking pattern, they think like the world and act like they have always acted yet their spirit has been reborn. The Bible refers to such as a soulish or carnal believer. They can be referred to as babes in Christ, who live more in the natural than in the spirit.

> *1 And I, brethren, could not speak unto you as unto spiritual, but as*
> *unto carnal, even as unto babes in Christ.*

1 Corinthians 3:1

Paul talked about this mind renewal in his letter to the

Romans, Corinthians and Colossians.

> ² *And be not conformed to this world: but be ye transformed by the renewing of your mind, that ye may prove what is that good, and acceptable, and perfect, will of God.*
>
> *Romans 12:2*

It is the renewing of your mind that transforms you and constrains you from operating in the world system. Look at the instruction to the Colossian Church.

> ¹⁰ *And have put on the new man, which is renewed in knowledge after the image of him that created him:*
>
> *Colossians 3:10*

Remember, old things have passed away and behold all things are new. Being a new creature, you are renewed in Christ in the full and true knowledge of who God is. You cannot afford to remain in a state of ignorance where your walk as a believer ends at accepting Jesus Christ. Salvation is just the beginning of the journey. You must seek to be transformed and renewed to be Christ like to empower you to live a victorious life.

The road to renewal and transformation is not an easy road to ply. Your flesh will have none of it and will wage all manner of war against you, trying to undo things that you have been doing for years that have now developed into habits. The flesh will resist change as much as it can get away with.

All manner of things will come at you just to make sure you do not leave the pit of sin and filth, but if you are so determined that you want to live the quality of life that your new nature brings even when you fall, you get up. It is not having the mindset that it is impossible, but believing that you can do all things through Christ who strengthens you. I used to think it was absolutely impossible for anyone to live a life that measures up to God's standard, but my pattern of thought was cured when I found out that it did not depend on me but on the power of the Holy Spirit that works in me. It then dawned on me that the scripture in Zechariah 4:6 *"not by power or might but by my Spirit saith the Lord"* means it is not by your works or your limited understanding you achieve anything but your leaning on the Holy Spirit to help you be all that you can be.

Loving others is a tough one. *How can you love someone who is obviously out to cause you harm and does not even care?* Yet, you are not allowed to take offense but love the person unconditionally. That sounds hilarious in your ears doesn't it?, But the truth is that you are meant to take the hurt, offense, negative feeling, annoyance, anger, irritation or what the issue is to God. It is really not by your power or might.

God surely knows what you are going through and how you feel, but He wants you to talk to Him about it as a child would tell a mother or father all the hurt felt, then ask for the burden to be lifted. It has worked for me time and time again; and you find out you can look at the person not from your human eyes but the eyes of God and know that there is room for such a person in your heart.

It all starts with the way you think. *Remember, as a man thinketh in his heart so is he.*

Power of Thoughts

Your thought life is very powerful, so powerful that the devil does not give your thought life breathing space. He knows that if you can think it, then you can do it. Once something enters your mind, it has a chance of coming to pass whether positive or negative. Creation itself is as a result of God's thought life. Let us go back to before the beginning of everything Genesis.

> ² *And the earth was without form, and void; and darkness was upon the face of the deep. And the Spirit of God moved upon the face of the waters.*
> ³ *And God said, Let there be light: and there was light.*

Genesis 1:2-3

Where did all of creation come from? Before creation or before the beginning took place, God must have taken His time to think up everything with detailed precision. He thought it well before He spoke it into being. We can see in *verse 3* where He pronounced purpose. The purpose of light was to eliminate darkness and bring clarity. Everything He created had a purpose. He did not just open His mouth and speak idle words, He put His rich imagination to work and birthed what you and I see today.

To really appreciate the power of God's thought life, you should study the account in *Job 38-42*. God speaking to Job asked him where he was when He the Lord laid the foundations of the earth (*Job 38:4*) or if Job knew where the light resides (*verse 19*) or if he has entered into the treasures of the snow or seen the treasures of the hail (*verse 22*). He questioned Job if he could send lightening on errands and they would respond and answer him here we are (*verse 35*) or if Job could bind the sweet influences of Pleiades or lose the bands of Orion (*verse 31*). *This is in reference to the constellations* or in *verse 8 and 11* where He shut the seas with doors and instructed it where to stop its waves from spreading further. I can go on and on. So you can understand the power of God's thoughts in bringing things into being. And in *Genesis 1:4*, He looked at what He had created and saw it was good.

Your Thoughts and You

The scripture says you are what you think, so what are the things that shape your thoughts?, What are the things that are your predominant thoughts? The things that have moulded you into who you are today and become your habit. The major things that shape your thinking pattern are;

- What you spend your time reading
- What you expose your eyes to, Television and Internet
- What you constantly listen to , radio and music
- Your environment
- The people you spend most of your time with
- Your Family.

There are other factors but I will only deal with the above mentioned. *What do you spend your time watching? It* is known as *'tell-a-vision'* (*telling your mind a vision*). The various media have a stronghold on the society today. The media consisting of Television, Internet, Radio and Print media have become the source of forming and reflecting public opinion. The Television and Internet channels have become very influential and controls the average person's life style. It dictates what is viewed and when it is viewed for most individuals. You may have the remote but the media corporations dictate the programmes. Tony Mandez reiterated this point in his article, where he stated that *"people have lost their souls to phantom delights such as films, soap operas, vanity shows, falling into stupor or apathetic hypnosis"* what Lazerfeld called *narcotizing dysfunction of exposure to mass media.* Media has created irrational victims of false wants. The wants which media corporations have thrust upon them and continue to do through advertisement.

I must say that I quite agree with him. A lot of people have formed their ideologies of what they should look like, walk like, talk like from the television, and anything short of that is below standard. You find young women who want to be as thin as the models seen on television or young men dressing like rap stars because they think it is hip. Media dictates fashion even in remote villages. People want to become what they see and not what they know. Self development is stalled and what we get now are more copies than originals.

As a believer what do you spend your time watching? The question is *"how profitable is that programme you spend your precious hours watching?"* It is called *tell-a-vision,* and it is the vision that speaks to your mind and forms a pattern which eventually grows into a way of thinking and then a habit is formed. What you expose yourself to watch frames your thought life, that is why Paul in *Romans 12:1-2* declares to believers *"not to be conformed to this world, meaning we are not to do things as the world does, but be transformed with the renewing of our minds..."*

I am not saying that nothing good comes out of the media. There are a lot of Christian programmes aired on the television from Christian channels that can help you get to the Word of God and help you build your knowledge in His Word.

How edifying are the things you listen to? Your mind forms its thoughts based on what you fill your ears with. Listening to the news these days, you discover that a significant percentage of the news reports are borderline negative. I remember a few years back I used to watch a lot of movies about slavery and all the things that went on in those plantations. It stirred up my emotions in a negative and resentful manner that it started to reflect in the way I thought and acted but thank God for the school of life and reality check called the Word of God. I would probably be in a very deep and strong bondage today. The effects of what you watch and listen to gradually manifests itself in your speech and action.

The advent of the Internet has even made it worse. *Blogging, Twittering, Facebooking* for hours unending. How does this profit you? Some people can spend four hours facebooking or twittering but the moment they are asked to pick up their Bible, they are burnt out within fifteen minutes dozing off or being distracted. How can we forget the *'mini tell-a-vision'* called the mobile phone, since the television is not mobile, a mobile phone is created where you have all the works of a television. This is constantly keep you occupied that you have very little time left for the things of God.

I am trying to open your eyes to how these seemingly inconsequential things can become devices of the enemy. The Bible says in *2 Corinthians 2:11 "lest satan should take advantage of us: we are not ignorant of his devices"*, he has enslaved many with gadgets and has kept them from knowing the truth which would set them free for life. This may sound fanatical but Jesus is looking for genuine fanatics.

If Jesus did not come across as a fanatic and sweated blood for you and I to have life after death, then who else should be a fanatic if not you and I. Jesus did not care what anyone had to say about His mission of salvation, so why should you care about what anyone says. Until you reach the level in your life where it is all about Jesus, then are you really ready to walk the walk?. Television is infiltrated with sexual themes and profanity, even the *PG* rated movies have hidden sexual contexts. Some of the movies our precious children watch always end up with the main characters kissing and living happily ever after. Then you wonder why your two year old is filled with curiosity and wanting to kiss everything that walks by. At that early age, they are already exposed and such thoughts are deeply rooted in their minds and you wonder why at the age of six they want to experiment.

One has to be careful what we allow filter into our minds because whatever gets into our minds dominates our lives. We are instructed in *Philippians 4:8* to think on things that are true, honest, just, pure, lovely, of good report. Things that have virtue and are praise worthy. Remember, the issues of life flow from your heart.

The Power of Thinking Right

As previously discussed, we saw how God exercised His thought life and brought about creation. If you remember, in *Genesis 1:26,* you were created in His image and likeness. He bestowed you with a rich mind that can set itself up to achieve anything you want it to. I have come to realise that the way we think is what determines how we perceive and react to things. You often hear motivational speakers talking about visualizing all that you want to see take place in your life. It is the same principle. What does your mind's eye see? How far can your mind visualize? These are called imaginations. It is forming mental images, creating concepts that are not seen physically but are capable of being brought into existence. You can only attain in life what your mind can see. God used this concept of imaginations in several places in the Bible.

Firstly, we see in *Genesis 13:14-18* where He told Abraham to expand his mind's eye when He asked him to lift up his eyes and look north, south, east and west and all that he could see will be given to Abraham's seed.

> *¹⁴ And the LORD said unto Abram, after that Lot was separated from him, Lift up now thine eyes, and look from the place where thou art northward, and southward, and eastward, and westward:*
> *¹⁵ For all the land which thou seest, to thee will I give it, and to thy seed for ever.*
> *¹⁶ And I will make thy seed as the dust of the earth: so that if a man can number the dust of the earth, then shall thy seed also be numbered.*
> *¹⁷ Arise, walk through the land in the length of it and in the breadth of it; for I will give it unto thee.*
> *¹⁸ Then Abram removed his tent, and came and dwelt in the plain of Mamre, which is in Hebron, and built there an altar unto the LORD.*
>
> *Genesis 13:14-18*

This action spurred Abraham as we see in *verse 18*, he moved his tent towards the place of promise. Again Abraham gets schooled when he was instructed in *Genesis 15:5*.

> *⁵ Then he took him outside and said, "Look at the sky. Count the stars. Can you do it? Count your descendants! You're going to have a big family, Abram!"*
>
> *Genesis 15:5 (MSG)*

God did this to expand Abraham's mind to think big and to think outside the box, not limiting himself in his thoughts, and making him exercise his mind. Show me a man with a vision and you have a man on a mission.

Another beautiful illustration I like very much is the story in *Ezekiel 37:1-14*. Here, the prophet Ezekiel was taken up by the Spirit of God to a valley of dry bones and the Lord asked Ezekiel if it was possible for the dry bones to rise up again. He wanted him to exercise his mind and strengthen his faith because the lesson to learn here is that, with God nothing, absolutely nothing is impossible. He instructs Ezekiel to speak to the bones to come alive and they did. Three things took place *see it, think it and speak it.* Thank God. Ezekiel was smart enough to answer that it was only God who knew for a fact if the dead dried up bones could live or not.

There is another example worth looking at. Twelve spies were sent out into the land of Canaan to view what the land looked like and what was going on there. Of the twelve sent out, only two could see outright victory over the giants that occupied the promised land. Because of how the spies saw themselves, none of the ten entered into the promised land. It is interesting to note that the things they were sore afraid of, were afraid of them too. It is the same thing with believers who are afraid to take hold of their lives when the world is sore afraid of them manifesting their God given power.

In every promise land or desired future, there will be giants or obstacles that do not want you to possess what is yours. The good news is this; these giants are afraid of you because they know the Name by which you come and the power that works in you. They intimidate you with size but you petrify them with the power of God that dwells in you. How can size match power? Face every opposition with boldness because God has already given you victory. God is saying you should go there and make a show out of them. God is backing you and no one can be against you.

Your thoughts are your unspoken words, your imagination is a series of words put together in a graphic sense, this is where inventions are created, paintings are drawn, books are written, and architecture is created. These thoughts are what motivates you to achieve things in life that no one else has. The greatest achievements in life started from the point of imagination. Imagine yourself living a victorious life with your new identity.

A person with a rich mind never runs out of ideas. What do you see in your mind's eye about your future? When you are in tuned with the Lord, He gives you inspirations that burn in your mind. When you act in line with this inspiration, you create something great.

> [17] *Thus says the Lord, your Redeemer, the Holy One of Israel: I am the Lord your God, Who teaches you to profit, Who leads you in the way that you should go.*
>
> *Isaiah 48:17 (AMP)*

God fills your mind with thoughts far bigger than anything you could have ever thought of, that may seem impossible to achieve, but it motivates you to go all out to see it come to pass.

> [27] *And Jesus looking upon them saith, With men it is impossible, but not with God: for with God all things are possible.*
>
> *Mark 10:27*

Inspirational thoughts are God finding expression for His will through the minds of human beings. You have to be careful what you think, negative thoughts will materialize negative results. Your failure or success in life starts from your thoughts, so you cannot afford to have a stinking thought life as Joyce Meyer put it. What you think determines what comes out of your mouth and that limits the potential God has placed in you.

Thoughts should be inspired by the word of God. This

is why you are instructed by God to meditate on them, pondering deeply and soaking your mind in the Word of God. Visualise all the promises God has made available to you. If He says you are blessed, what do imagine the blessings to be? Think big, have lofty thoughts, think far, think the impossible because with God they are possible. Do you think you are a success or a failure? How do you perceive yourself?, What do you want to become in life, what is your mental image? Dare to dream big.

Improve your thinking. Set your thoughts on great things, be optimistic, do not let negative circumstances deter you from seeing and believing. Always put your thoughts in check. Do not let negative thoughts filter and dwell in your heart. You have the mind of Christ and therefore an excellent spirit is upon you to achieve all things. Take steps to put your thoughts into action. It is not just thinking it, you need to act it.

Train your mind to think right, focusing on the Word of God. Your success in this world depends on what the Word of God says concerning you. When you are faced with problems in life, what determines the action you take? Are you ruled by your thoughts and emotions, do you let your emotions drive you? Do you waste time *feeling* the problem or do you take authority of the situation with what the Word of God says? You are to apply the Word of God to the situation because it is the Word of God that will set you free.

The devils greatest weapon is suggestions. He pervades your mind with suggestions which are contrary to the Word of God but appeals to the mind and conscience. Out of lack of a better understanding, you mull over these suggestions which by now are thoughts and the more time you spend contemplating these thoughts the stronger the hold they have and they become what is known as strongholds. I had a very interesting definition of what I thought strongholds were, I always thought they were demonic oppressions that a person was under, where large, strong, fierce demons held one captive and were constantly on guard, making it impossible to do anything about it, but praise God for wisdom, understanding and revelation knowledge.

Strongholds are nothing but wrong thoughts that are contrary to the word of God, that have become a thinking pattern and way of life that is difficult to break. These are thoughts that have never been challenged or disputed, usually thoughts from experiences, family beliefs passed down from generations and many other sources. I have put it in the very simplistic terms but more often than not, wrong thoughts have been given free reign to build a fortified city in your mind becoming a way of life which produces wrong results.

Let us look at an example. John is a clumsy person and often breaking things or knocking things over, maybe because he has long legs and household items get destroyed. His mother keeps cursing at him with words such as *"clumsy fool"*, *"everything you touch ends up being destroyed"* *"you cannot do anything good with yourself apart from destroying things"*, *"you have a destructive spirit"*, John is constantly exposed to such words, then he grows into a fine young man but feels very insecure about his physique, to others he looks perfect but to him he thinks his long legs are a curse to him because of what he went through as a child. In him is the ability to excel in track and field events because he has what it takes to excel in long jump, but nothing he is told will ever make him go to the fields and practise, now he has short changed himself and the world from enjoying the mastery of his talent.

Every time he is told how he could do well in sports, the devil will always remind him of his mothers words, the words have become a strong hold in his life and those thoughts went uncontested for years. It brought in fear which has become the king in his life, incapacitating his mind and body. He wishes to do many things but they end as just wishes. Help is here because God has given us the cure for strongholds.

> *3 For though we walk (live) in the flesh, we are not carrying on our warfare according to the flesh and using mere human weapons.*
> *4 For the weapons of our warfare are not physical [weapons of flesh and blood], but they are mighty before God for the overthrow and destruction of strongholds,*
> *5 [Inasmuch as we] refute arguments and theories and reasonings and every proud and lofty thing that sets itself up against the [true] knowledge of God; and we lead every thought and purpose away captive into the obedience of Christ (the Messiah, the Anointed One).*
>
> *2 Corinthians 10:3-5 (AMP)*

Firstly you must understand that you do not battle against physical things, the war is not against any human being. Human beings are merely instruments used by the devil. Your fight is against principalities and rulers of darkness, wicked spirits that bring suggestions into your mind that lead you into captivity and bondage. These captivities are not physical either, you are not tied up in chains, you walk around, go about your daily business but you live a life of self doubt, worthlessness and failure.

> *10-12 And that about wraps it up. God is strong, and he wants you strong. So take everything the Master has set out for you, well-made weapons of the best materials. And put them to use so you will be able to stand up to everything the Devil throws your way. This is no afternoon athletic contest that we'll walk away from and forget about in a couple of hours. This is for keeps, a life-or-death fight to the finish*

against the Devil and all his angels.

13-18 Be prepared. You're up against far more than you can handle on your own. Take all the help you can get, every weapon God has issued, so that when it's all over but the shouting you'll still be on your feet. Truth, righteousness, peace, faith, and salvation are more than words. Learn how to apply them. You'll need them throughout your life. God's Word is an indispensable weapon. In the same way, prayer is essential in this ongoing warfare. Pray hard and long. Pray for your brothers and sisters. Keep your eyes open. Keep each other's spirits up so that no one falls behind or drops out.

Ephesians 6:11-18 (MSG)

The sum of all of the above is that the battle is not against flesh and blood but against principalities, against powers, against the rulers of darkness of this world, against spiritual wickedness in high places, not the people you see but evil spirits that are unseen. You now can appreciate that these are not going to let you have breathing space, they want to ensure that your life is a mockery.

As stated above, the Word of God is indispensable. The weapon for dealing with undisputed thoughts and suggestions that have formed strongholds is the Word of Truth. You cannot fight these reasoning's, teachings, traditions, customs, fables, superstitions, doctrines, high systems of ethics, philosophies that oppose the truth and contradict the Word of God that have found refuge in our minds with your physical powers but with the powers made available to you by God to destroy. We take thoughts captive by bringing them captive to the obedience of Christ, making a fool of these thoughts with the Word of Truth.

The way to capture every wrong thought with the Word of God is to pronounce the Truth. Declare the word of truth according to what is written in the Bible. You cannot afford to keep quiet, you must assert the words loudly. Declare it. Do not permit or tolerate the thought. Break the backbone of the thought with the Word of God.

Take for instance a thought comes to your mind that you are a failure and cannot pass whatever task that is before you, present the word of truth by declaring immediately that *"I am not a failure but a success, I excel in all that I do, I have an excellent spirit upon me"* You can find the scripture in *Daniel 4*. You always have to always assert your stance with scriptures. Repeat it constantly and do not relent in your fight. Negative thoughts are always countered by positive speaking. This simple exercise automatically breaks the chain of negative thoughts and brings your mind to absorb the truth. Alternatively pray in tongues.

God did not create a failure or a loser. When He created you He said you are good *Genesis 1:31*. If He looked at you and said you are good with mighty potentials, it is left to you to harness your thoughts and make good use of all that has been deposited in you. Deal with doubts and fears with the Word of God.

God desires for us all to live a life of possibilities and not a life of limitations. Resist helplessness and depression, adopt a high level of enthusiasm, take responsibility for your actions. Always create new opportunities for yourself. Visualize the future. Be a visionary.

Chapter Summary

What we hear people speak about is what they have been thinking about.

Strongholds are nothing but wrong thoughts that are contrary to the word of God that have become a thinking pattern and way of life that is difficult to break.

God desires for us all to live a life of possibilities and not a life of limitations.

Negative thoughts are always countered by positive speaking.

Chapter 11

I Have What I Say

*F*rom the last chapter, you should now understand the power the mind has in controlling the rest of the body. Your actions are controlled by what you think and your thoughts are controlled by what you believe. *Matthew 12:34 says "for out of the fullness, the over flow, the superabundance of the heart the mouth speaks"*. There is tremendous power in spoken words. Right thinking produces right speaking that leads to the right attitude and right decisions. Words have potent power. See how Paul describes the Word of God

> [12] *For the Word that God speaks is alive and full of power [making it active, operative, energizing, and effective]; it is sharper than any two-edged sword, penetrating to the dividing line of the [a]breath of life (soul) and [the immortal] spirit, and of joints and marrow [of the deepest parts of our nature], exposing and sifting and analyzing and judging the very thoughts and purposes of the heart.*
>
> *Hebrews 4:12 (AMP)*

See the words used to describe God's Word. *Alive, full of*

power, energising, operative, effective, penetrating, exposing.
These descriptions show how deep the word of God can go
and how effective it is. It knows your desires, your passions
and all the hidden things that the outward man cannot see.

What have my words go to do with it?

The words of man equally have power because God had
from the onset breathe His Spirit in us and created man in
His image and likeness. Man is supposed to represent God
here on earth but a lot of us do not realise the effects our
words have to us and to the world at large. The book of
Proverbs 18:12 tells us that *"death and life are in the power of
the tongue, and they that love it shall eat the fruit thereof"*. What
this passage is simply saying is that the words of your
mouth determine your success or failure. The power of
the tongue if put to right use will yield life. You are either
justified or condemned by the words of your mouth. There
are two things here;

- Words are extremely important and
- You are the one who has the power to determine
  the words you speak.

Webster's standard dictionary defines *"word"* as *"the
smallest meaningful unit of language, speech, a brief remark,
message, comment, command etc, a promise, verbal oral
communications (word of mouth)"*. I am certain you have
read books on the power of words. Well, these books or
teachings are very important. It is an opportunity to let
you realize the damage we cause in our lives because of
the wrong answers and wrong words we speak.

There is tremendous power in the words you speak.

   [11] *If any man speak, let him speak as the oracles of God; if any man*

minister, let him do it as of the ability which God giveth: that God in all things may be glorified through Jesus Christ, to whom be praise and dominion for ever and ever. Amen.

1 Peter 4:11

Peter urges us to speak as the oracles of God, pure in speech. Paul also identified these oracles in the his letter to the Romans.

² Much every way: chiefly, because that unto them were committed the oracles of God.

Romans 3:2

As a child of God you are His oracle, speaking His word and professing what ought to be.

My word the Seed

Jesus, in teaching on the word, used many illustrations with seeds. He likened words to seeds. A good example is the parable of the sower in *Matthew 13:3-32*. In *verse 18*, He illustrated the word of God as a seed planted on several grounds. Some yielded fruits while some did not even make it at all. The words you speak are seeds that you plant and will certainly develop into a fruit bearing plant or weed. When you talk and say things, do not assume that they are lost words. There is an adage which says that *words are like eggs, once broken it cannot be mended, once said cannot be taken back*. *Proverbs 18:20* states that *"you are satisfied with the fruit of your mouth, and with the increase of your lips shall you be saved."*

² A man shall eat good by the fruit of his mouth: but the soul of the transgressors shall eat violence.
³ He that keepeth his mouth keepeth his life: but he that openeth wide his lips shall have destruction.

Proverbs 13:2-3

Verse 3 says that if you keep your mouth, you keep your life, but destruction befalls those who cannot take charge of their mouths. What is being said here is for you to watch your words. If you want to achieve anything in life, your disposition is what determines the word that comes out of you. If you enjoy speaking negative things into your life, it is because your mind is filled with negative thoughts. You cannot expect to enjoy the benefits of positive thinking, when you sow negative words into your life. You may not immediately see the results of your words, but it is growing and working towards its manifestation. If you speak positive words that are inclined to the will of God, you will reap the harvest of the positive things you have sown into your life.

The question that comes to mind now is what kind of words do I speak and what words make up my vocabulary? As you sow in the word so will you reap in the word. Human beings have the tendency to pick up wrong words and slogans, words that do not help you in anyway. Take stock of the things you say, take stock of the words that appeal to you, then you can determine the type of things you unconsciously say. Often times mothers say negative things to their children in a moment of irritation or when a child is acting badly. They use derogatory words such as *failure, no good, useless, good for nothing, incapable, bastards, vagabond* etc. The child grows up to be exactly what you have spoken him/her to be. Even if your child is doing averagely in his or her studies, rather than voice your disappointment by calling your child names, speak encouraging words and prophesy words such as *"you have an excellent spirit to excel in all things, and not just in your academics, you are fearfully and wonderfully made in the image and likeness if God, or you have the mind of Christ."* There are more than enough positive words to sow into your children and anything else for that matter.

Do not empower the spirit of failure with your words, remember your words have life in them and whatever you say empowers the spirit behind the words. Excellence has a spirit *"the spirit of excellence"*, death *"the spirit of death"*, life *"the spirit of life"*, lack *"the spirit of lack"*, sorrow *"the spirit of sorrow"*, heaviness *"the spirit of heaviness"* etc, . It is very important for you to know that the spirit realm controls the physical and there is nothing physical that does not have a spiritual equivalent.

My words and the Spirit realm

We must have knowledge and understanding of the spirit realm and how it affects our lives. The God we serve who is our Father, is a spirit being and not a physical being. We relate with Him through the spirit.

> [24] *God is a Spirit: and they that worship him must worship him in spirit and in truth.*

> *John 4:24*

He is a person with a personal spirit, soul and body, the difference between God's nature and man's nature is that He does not inhabit this body of clay called flesh. He is of a spirit substance *Hebrew 1:3*. He has hands, legs, mouth, lips, everything. Remember you are created in likeness and His image *Genesis 1:26*. The kingdom of God and Heaven are all in the spirit realm. In *Luke 10:21,* Jesus is recorded rejoicing in the spirit, thanking God who is the Lord of Heaven and earth. The earth is the physical realm that you can see and the dwelling for human beings while Heaven is the dwelling place of the Most High God. The spirit realm is there and is more powerful, more living than most of us could ever fathom. It can only be seen with the eye of faith.

Faith is believing that everything that we need or want already exists in the spirit realm. The things you are hoping for are in the store house of Heaven even though you cannot see them with your physical eyes. We believe the wind exists, yet none of us has ever seen the wind. All the blessings you will need in your life time are already piled up for you waiting to be claimed. Heaven is not just going to manufacture blessings. Everything you will ever need it is already there. Healing, deliverance, breakthrough etc. are all there right now as you read this book.

Bringing the Spiritual into the Physical

There are two things that are crucial if we want to succeed in bringing the spiritual into the physical. These are *Faith* and *Words*. In order words, spiritual things enter the physical world through speaking faith filled words. This is why the Bible says you are snared by the words of your mouth. You either destroy or keep alive all that concerns you through your words.

Two types of kingdoms exist in the spirit realm, the kingdom of God and the kingdom of darkness. The kingdom of God rules over everything but the kingdom of darkness tries to pervert the workings of the kingdom of God. While God issues out blessings to you, the kingdom of darkness will do everything to withhold it so that you think God does not want to bless you.

The way things are done in the spirit realm is far different from how things are done in the physical. As a believer you are not of this world but only live in the world to fulfil a purpose after which you return to the spirit realm. Both Heaven and Hell are in the spirit realm where conscious realities exist. The existence of earth today is the manifestation of what God spoke into being in *Genesis 1*. Everything is a product of the spirit realm, and it had been in existence way before the earth was created.

> [3] *By faith we understand that the universe was formed at God's command, so that what is seen was not made out of what was visible.*
>
> Hebrews 11:3 (Today's New International Version, ©2005)

Remember man is made of three components-: the body (*flesh*), the soul (*intellect, will, emotions, thoughts*), and the spirit. We are all spirit beings living in a body of flesh and God is the Father of all spirits (*Hebrew 12:9*). When God wants something done in the physical, He speaks in Heaven and someone on earth with hear that voice and release it into the atmosphere. Once those words are released, they cannot return without bringing forth results.

Your physical mind is limited in a lot of ways that you do not see by your understanding. But as a believer, God renews your mind so that you can think and see beyond your human understanding. He expands the scope of your horizon far beyond the physical. There is more to life than what we see. Once you can grasp faith, you have automatically stepped up into God's playing field. You have simply removed yourself from your physical limitations as a man and have moved up to doing things, thinking things, and obtaining things in the spirit realm.

Your words are amplified in the spirit realm. The words you speak in the physical are the activation key to the spiritual. You cannot think the spirit realm into being, you speak it into being. You are really justified by the words of your mouth and a careless promise made in the physical is taken seriously in the spiritual, that is why Jesus said in *Matthew 12:36* that *"you will give account for every idle word you speak on the day of judgment."*

God is bound by His words and so are we.

> [2] Be not rash with thy mouth, and let not thine heart be hasty to utter any thing before God: for God is in heaven, and thou upon earth: therefore let thy words be few.
> [3] For a dream cometh through the multitude of business; and a fool's voice is known by multitude of words.
> [4] When thou vowest a vow unto God, defer not to pay it; for he hath no pleasure in fools: pay that which thou hast vowed.
> [5] Better is it that thou shouldest not vow, than that thou shouldest vow and not pay.

Ecclesiastes 5:2-5

Verse 2 says "don't shoot off your mouth, or speak before you think. Don't be too quick to tell God what you think He wants to hear. God is in charge and not you- the less you speak, the better." God never contradicts Himself. I have never read or come across any scripture where God declares Himself as *"a fool"*, *"failure"*, *"good for nothing"*, *"sleaze"*, *"low life"*, *"incapable"*, *"inferior"*. The list is endless but these words make up the vocabulary of a lot of believers. Though we are made in His image and likeness, the devil has fooled us long enough because he knows that we are ensnared by the words of our mouth. Our vocabulary consist of so much more negative words than positive.

> [20] A man's belly shall be satisfied with the fruit of his mouth; and with the increase of his lips shall he be filled.

Proverbs 18:20

So the more good words you speak, the more good fruits you will reap. The more bad words you speak, the more bad fruits you reap. You either live or die depending on your mind and mouth. The things that come out of it will make you or break you. A good example of those who killed their destiny with their mouths are the ten spies out of twelve in *Numbers 14:36-37,* who had a negative report about the land. It was only Caleb and Joshua that had positive things to say and they entered into the promise of their inheritance. *James 3:5-9* gives us a clear picture of the nature of the tongue and it's power.

> ⁵ Even so the tongue is a little member, and boasteth great things. Behold, how great a matter a little fire kindleth!
> ⁶ And the tongue is a fire, a world of iniquity: so is the tongue among our members, that it defileth the whole body, and setteth on fire the course of nature; and it is set on fire of hell.
> ⁷ For every kind of beasts, and of birds, and of serpents, and of things in the sea, is tamed, and hath been tamed of mankind:
> ⁸ But the tongue can no man tame; it is an unruly evil, full of deadly poison.
> ⁹ Therewith bless we God, even the Father; and therewith curse we men, which are made after the similitude of God.
>
> *James 3:5-9*

It is pertinent that you refrain your tongue from evil and your lips from speaking guile or deceitful or treacherous things. Keep your mouth and if you do, you keep your life (*Proverbs 13:3*) and you keep your soul from trouble (*Proverbs 21:23*). Understand one thing, you cannot tame your tongue, but you can ask the Holy Spirit to help you speak the right words.

> ³ Set a watch, O LORD, before my mouth; keep the door of my lips.
>
> *Psalm 141:3*

David is calling on God to keep watch over his mouth and keep a door over his lips. This is very important because it will stop you from using wrong words to bring your life to a halt. Keep filthy communications away from your mouth (*Ephesians 4:29*). Use your mouth to bless yourself and others. Do not be unstable with your words. Groom your words to be positive words. Your words contain power so use the power for yourself and not against yourself.

Assert the word of God into your life. Invoke God's blessings into your life, speak out the promises of God concerning you, start your day by infusing the atmosphere with the word of God. Determine your day by taking authority over it and saturating it with the favour, terminating the purpose of the enemies concerning your day. Doing this automatically affects you. Speak favour, peace, breakthroughs, abundance, open doors into your day. Discipline yourself to command your morning everyday. Use your mouth wisely, it is the gateway to light or darkness. Your day is charged by how you set it.

Never start your day without invoking powerful scriptures into it. It may sound like you are being silly but your silliness is your victory over the forces of darkness. There are uncountable blessings in the Bible. Train your tongue to speak these words until it becomes part of you and a way of life for you. You put the days problems at bay when you sow God's words into your day and life. You are establishing the will of God and He has no choice but to honour His words. This is one powerful tool that the enemy does not want you to know so that he can continue to bind you through your words and constantly accuse you.

Fear and your words

Fear is a very strong factor that affects your word life and your life in general. Fear cripples, incapacitates and deters you from speaking with authority. When fear is present in your life, it breeds negativity and will never allow you to see anything positive to speak about. Fear can be caused by a number of things which include rejection, hurtful words and negative experiences. A negative thought life is a negative word life.

> *⁷ For God did not give us a spirit of timidity (of cowardice, of craven and cringing and fawning fear), but [He has given us a spirit] of power and of love and of calm and well-balanced mind and discipline and self-control.*

2 Timothy 1:7 (AMP)

If you live in fear you do not possess a sound mind. With a sound mind, you can think and command power. *1 John 4:18* says there is no fear in love, but perfect love casts out all fear. Fear is a torment. He that fears is not made perfect in love, and *1 John 4:8* says that God is love, therefore fear will not make you perfect in God, and you cannot operate in power with a tormented mind. Deal with fear and get rid of it at all cost. As said earlier, when dealing with any situation, you must understand their nature and origin. Most things have a spirit behind them. Fear is no exception. Fear is a spirit, *2 Timothy 1:7* lets us know that *"God has not given you the spirit of fear..."* so in dealing with the spirit of fear you must know the scripture in (*Ephesians 6:11-17*). With fear, you are not wrestling against flesh and blood but against principalities, powers and rulers of darkness, and spiritual wickedness.

You need to put on all the armour of warfare which is truth, righteousness, the gospel of peace, faith and salvation. Without these weapons, you cannot achieve anything in the spirit realm.

> *³ For though we walk in the flesh, we do not war after the flesh:*
> *⁴ (For the weapons of our warfare are not carnal, but mighty through God to the pulling down of strong holds;)*
> *⁵ Casting down imaginations, and every high thing that exalteth itself against the knowledge of God, and bringing into captivity every thought to the obedience of Christ;*
> *⁶ And having in a readiness to revenge all disobedience, when your obedience is fulfilled.*

2 Corinthians 10:3-6

Fear is not something you see, it is something you feel that is rooted in thoughts and imaginations. If you do not deal with the issue of fear in your life, it will lead you to confess negative things. The word of God is what eliminates fear. Your knowledge and belief in the Word of God will not allow you to entertain fear. You have not received the spirit of bondage to fear again but the spirit of adoption to cry Abba Father (*Romans 8:15*). Have the mindset of Christ, prophesy the word, confess it, cast down fear with the word of God. Let your mouth speak wisdom (*Psalms 49:3*), the Lord has given you a mouth and wisdom that your enemies cannot gainsay or resist (*Luke 21:15*). Use your mouth to speak deliverance and breakthrough from bondage. Your words are incubators carrying purpose and potentials in them.

Proverbs 6:12-15 clearly speaks about a man who devices evil, who walks with a forward mouth, an untamed and perverse mouth and his words are deceit. The result of all these is that calamity shall suddenly come and he shall be broken without remedy. The mouth opens the door to the evil one to do things that are inconsistent to the plan of God for your life. Use your mouth well. Go through the scriptures and write out as many promises contained there for your life, and make a habit of confessing them into your life. You can never go wrong with this because you are engaging God's word. A lot of blessings have passed us by because of ignorance. *Hosea 4:6* says "*we perish because we lack knowledge.*"

Matthew 6:33 says "*seek the Kingdom of God and His righteousness, and all these other things shall be added unto you.*" If you do not seek God, how then can you have anything added to you? *Job 22:26-29* says that we should "*delight in the Almighty and when you pray to Him, He will hear you. When you decree a thing it shall be established unto you and the light shall shine always upon your ways and when all men say there is a casting down, you will say there is a lifting up"*. This is the promise for those who know their God, and *Daniel 11:32* says that *"the people that know their God shall be strong and do exploits"*.

Chapter Summary

Your actions are controlled by what you think and your thoughts are controlled by what you believe.

The words you speak are seeds that you plant and will certainly develop into a fruit bearing plant or weed.

Keep your mouth and if you do, you keep your life

Your words contain power so use the power for yourself and not against yourself.

Chapter 12

The High Calling

*B*y now, from all we have said, I believe you should have a good understanding of who you really are in God and should be able to declare boldly, in faith, what God says about you. You are a child of God, a co-heir with Christ in our heavenly Father. You are created in the image and likeness of God and now have a right relationship with Him. You are a new creation, a chosen generation, a royal priesthood, a holy nation created for His praise and worship. You are God's master piece, the light of the world and the salt of the earth, chosen and called by God. You are a complete individual in Christ Jesus and you are a friend of God. If these words describe you, which they do, then you must be valuable. Now, everything of value has a purpose waiting to be discovered. What then is this calling?

A call is really just a stirring up for action. It is a request to adopt a thought, position or certain behavioural characteristics to bring you to a desired end. The call of God for us has not changed from the one He gave in the beginning. It is the call to fully exercise our original mandate to dominate, subdue and replenish, multiply in the earth.

> *28And God blessed them, and God said unto them, Be fruitful, and multiply, and replenish the earth, and subdue it: and have dominion over the fish of the sea, and over the fowl of the air, and over every living thing that moveth upon the earth.*
>
> *Genesis 1:28*

To fully understand the calling and exercise some of the benefits of it, I think it is important to remind ourselves what gives the calling a sure foundation.

Firstly, the calling is based on a covenant which cannot be broken. Why can the covenant not be broken? Well, covenant's by nature are based on a promise and require at least two parties before being called a covenant. It is a commitment by those involved to follow a particular course of action should a predetermined situation occur. This predetermined situation is usually the death of one of the parties. The key points here being the promise, the parties and the predetermined situation. Remember the promise is found in *Galatians 3:13-14 and Hebrews 6:13-20.*

> *13Christ hath redeemed us from the curse of the law, being made a curse for us: for it is written, Cursed is every one that hangeth on a tree:*
> *14That the blessing of Abraham might come on the Gentiles through Jesus Christ; that we might receive the promise of the Spirit through faith.*
>
> *Galatians 3:13-14*

> *13For when God made promise to Abraham, because he could swear by no greater, he sware by himself,*
> *14Saying, Surely blessing I will bless thee, and multiplying I will multiply thee.*
> *15And so, after he had patiently endured, he obtained the promise.*

> ¹⁶*For men verily swear by the greater: and an oath for confirmation is to them an end of all strife.*
> ¹⁷*Wherein God, willing more abundantly to shew unto the heirs of promise the immutability of his counsel, confirmed it by an oath:*
> ¹⁸*That by two immutable things, in which it was impossible for God to lie, we might have a strong consolation, who have fled for refuge to lay hold upon the hope set before us:*
> ¹⁹*Which hope we have as an anchor of the soul, both sure and stedfast, and which entereth into that within the veil;*
> ²⁰*Whither the forerunner is for us entered, even Jesus, made an high priest for ever after the order of Melchisedec.*

Hebrews 6:13-20

The parties are God the Father, Abraham and Jesus and the predetermined situation is the death of Jesus on the cross. Now, because Christ died on the Cross, we know the covenant has come into force and the covenant cannot be changed. Knowing that God cannot lie, the promise can be trusted.

> ²⁴*But this man, because he continueth ever, hath an unchangeable priesthood.*

Hebrews 7:24

As long as the One who promised lives on, the covenant remains in force and we are assured of the everlasting tenure of the covenant.

Secondly, access to the covenant is by inheritance. Inheritance is substance acquired by another's effort to which you have the rights of sonship to claim ownership. You need to understand the infallible nature of God and how He has made provisions for you, an eternal inheritance, that extends beyond this life time entitling you to citizenship in heaven. How do you know what is in the inheritance? You check the contents of the covenant. This is why we examined the Word of God in previous chapters. The word of God, the Bible, represents the words of the covenant. This is why the word of God is very important. Your success in life is not only determined by what is in the covenant. It is determined by the part of the covenant you know and execute. The knowledge of the covenant you have is what determines how you execute the calling. The knowledge of the covenant you have produces faith which is a requirement for a response from God as you cannot come to Him without faith.

It is important to know the place faith plays in the execution of calling. The calling is usually something you believe before any physical manifestation. You may not see it, but you know and believe that it exists. Believing in faith is one of the foundational keys to obtaining from God and one of the greatest investments you can make for yourself is to understand faith and how it operates. When faith is misunderstood or misapplied it leads to frustration. Faith is not about believing in an abstract thing. With faith, you believe in the words of a living God and you speak His words with authority, knowing you can count on Him to come through for you.

A clear understanding of faith is something every believer must have. There are many other practices of the believer that simply will not be effective without faith. Can you pray to Him without faith? Can you praise and worship Him without faith? Can you give thanks to Him without faith? Why do all these activities require faith? I hope you have noticed that they are all activities directed towards an unseen God. If it is seen with the natural senses, then it is not faith. So if prayer requires faith, then the believer must trust solely in the ability of God to execute the required action. Heaven only responds to the voice of faith. Christianity is based on believing the words of God as revealed to us in scriptures by the Holy Ghost. For example, every time you go to God in prayer believe that you have received your request even before you see any physical changes because what Jesus said was ask and it shall be given unto you.

> ⁷*Ask, and it shall be given you; seek, and ye shall find; knock, and it shall be opened unto you:*
> ⁸*For every one that asketh receiveth; and he that seeketh findeth; and to him that knocketh it shall be opened.*
> ⁹*Or what man is there of you, whom if his son ask bread, will he give him a stone?*
> ¹⁰*Or if he ask a fish, will he give him a serpent?*
> ¹¹*If ye then, being evil, know how to give good gifts unto your children, how much more shall your Father which is in heaven give good things to them that ask him?*
>
> *Matthew 7:7-11*

Everyone that asks shall receive, everyone that seeks shall find and everyone that knocks it shall be opened. Jesus did not say ask then wait for things to change before believing that He has answered your prayer. He said believe when you ask.

> ²⁴*Therefore I say unto you, What things soever ye desire, when ye pray, believe that ye receive them, and ye shall have them.*
>
> *Mark 11:24*

We need to train ourselves to walk by faith and not by sight. This means saying what God says about a situation and not what the facts of the situation may be telling you. Remember the story of Jesus and the daughter of a ruler of the synagogue in the gospels? Jesus could have agreed with the facts of the situation but He chose to go with His understanding of the will of God.

> ²²*And, behold, there cometh one of the rulers of the synagogue, Jairus by name; and when he saw him, he fell at his feet,*
> ²³*And besought him greatly, saying, My little daughter lieth at the point*

of death: I pray thee, come and lay thy hands on her, that she may be healed; and she shall live.

²⁴And Jesus went with him; and much people followed him, and thronged him.

Mark 5:22-24

³⁵While he yet spake, there came from the ruler of the synagogue's house certain which said, Thy daughter is dead: why troublest thou the Master any further?

³⁶As soon as Jesus heard the word that was spoken, he saith unto the ruler of the synagogue, Be not afraid, only believe.

³⁷And he suffered no man to follow him, save Peter, and James, and John the brother of James.

³⁸And he cometh to the house of the ruler of the synagogue, and seeth the tumult, and them that wept and wailed greatly.

³⁹And when he was come in, he saith unto them, Why make ye this ado, and weep? the damsel is not dead, but sleepeth.

⁴⁰And they laughed him to scorn. But when he had put them all out, he taketh the father and the mother of the damsel, and them that were with him, and entereth in where the damsel was lying.

⁴¹And he took the damsel by the hand, and said unto her, Talitha cumi; which is, being interpreted, Damsel, I say unto thee, arise.

⁴²And straightway the damsel arose, and walked; for she was of the age of twelve years. And they were astonished with a great astonishment.

⁴³And he charged them straitly that no man should know it; and commanded that something should be given her to eat.

Mark 5:35-43

Sometimes, the calling may lead you to walk against the tides of conventional wisdom but if you have the word of God in you, your mockers will be disappointed. As long as your continue making prophetic declarations, that is, confessions of the revelation of the word of God that the holy Spirit has put in your heart, you will reap your harvest of blessings. This is a law of God.

²²While the earth remaineth, seedtime and harvest, and cold and heat, and summer and winter, and day and night shall not cease.

Genesis 8:22

Notice that seedtime and harvest simply implies that you need to sow something and wait for a harvest. Sowing is firstly about speaking words before any action is taken. Your words are influential and powerful and are full of power to change your destiny for good. The word of God in your mouth will cause you soar above any situation in the earth.

You may say but I have been speaking the word of God but nothing has happened. Keep speaking it until something happens. If you keep speaking the word of God, whatever the word demands will ultimately come to pass. You make declarations from the revelation of the word of God in your heart, seeking diligently and knocking until the door is opened and you gain entrance. Do not give up on your request. It is God's will for you to enjoy all that He has in store for you.

This perseverance of faith is also demonstrated by God our Father. Do you realise that almost every prophet in the old testament spoke about the coming of Jesus? For thousands of years, God kept speaking through the prophets until one day, an angel of the Lord appeared unto Mary and the Word of God took on a physical form. This war of words is a vital part of spiritual warfare.

Enablers of The Calling

Once you have decided to take action in line with the calling, there are certain things you need to be aware of. These are things that create the right environment for your calling to flourish and produce the right results. A farmer that plants seeds needs to pay as much attention to the environment as he does to the seed he is planting. Seeds can die, not because the seed is bad but because the environment was not favourable. A lot of people have godly dreams but live by earthly standards thereby constraining the gift of God.

Let us look at some of these vital enablers.

The Holy Spirit

You cannot interpret your destiny by yourself. Without the Holy Spirit, you are vulnerable. You need the Holy spirit in everything. Every true calling starts with the Holy Spirit and we have to learn to lean on Him for help. The Holy Spirit was right there in the beginning of creation.

> *¹ In the beginning God created the heaven and the earth.*
> *² And the earth was without form, and void; and darkness was upon the face of the deep. And the Spirit of God moved upon the face of the waters.*
> *³ And God said, Let there be light: and there was light.*
>
> *Genesis 1:1-3*

He was there at the birth of Jesus and at every step of the way during his earthly assignment.

> *³⁰ And the angel said unto her, Fear not, Mary: for thou hast found favour with God.*
> *³¹ And, behold, thou shalt conceive in thy womb, and bring forth a son, and shalt call his name JESUS.*
> *³² He shall be great, and shall be called the Son of the Highest: and the Lord God shall give unto him the throne of his father David:*
> *³³ And he shall reign over the house of Jacob for ever; and of his kingdom there shall be no end.*
> *³⁴ Then said Mary unto the angel, How shall this be, seeing I know not a man?*
> *³⁵ And the angel answered and said unto her, The Holy Ghost shall come upon thee, and the power of the Highest shall overshadow thee: therefore also that holy thing which shall be born of thee shall be called the Son of God.*
>
> *Luke 1:30-35*

He was also there when the disciples of Jesus started out on there own after the resurrection of Jesus. They had to wait for Him. A lot of believers hear the call of God but they run ahead of the Spirit and fall flat on their faces.

> *46 And said unto them, Thus it is written, and thus it behooved Christ to suffer, and to rise from the dead the third day:*
> *47 And that repentance and remission of sins should be preached in his name among all nations, beginning at Jerusalem.*
> *48 And ye are witnesses of these things.*
> *49 And, behold, I send the promise of my Father upon you: BUT TARRY YE IN THE CITY OF JERUSALEM, UNTIL YE BE ENDUED WITH POWER FROM ON HIGH.*
>
> Luke 24:46-49

The Holy Spirit was again present at the beginning of the ministry of Paul.

> *13 Then Ananias answered, Lord, I have heard by many of this man, how much evil he hath done to thy saints at Jerusalem:*
> *14 And here he hath authority from the chief priests to bind all that call on thy name.*
> *15 But the Lord said unto him, Go thy way: for he is a chosen vessel unto me, to bear my name before the Gentiles, and kings, and the children of Israel:*
> *16 For I will shew him how great things he must suffer for my name's sake.*
> *17 And Ananias went his way, and entered into the house; and putting his hands on him said, BROTHER SAUL, THE LORD, EVEN JESUS, THAT APPEARED UNTO THEE IN THE WAY AS THOU CAMEST, HATH SENT ME, THAT THOU MIGHTEST RECEIVE THY SIGHT, AND BE FILLED WITH THE HOLY GHOST.*
> *18 And immediately there fell from his eyes as it had been scales: and he received sight forthwith, and arose, and was baptized.*
> *19 And when he had received meat, he was strengthened. Then was Saul certain days with the disciples which were at Damascus.*
> *20 AND STRAIGHTWAY HE PREACHED CHRIST IN*

THE SYNAGOGUES, *that he is the Son of God.*

Acts 9:10-20

So you really have to lean on the Holy Spirit to help you out, He anoints you , empowers you and reveals all things to you. It is the Holy Spirit behind the Word of God that makes the word powerful. He is the power behind the scenes that drives everything.

> *6 Then he answered and spake unto me, saying, This is the word of the LORD unto Zerubbabel, saying, Not by might, nor by power, but by my spirit, saith the LORD of hosts.*

Zechariah 4:6

It is the Holy Spirit that turns your effort into productivity. Paul said in *1 Corinthians 4:20,* the kingdom of the God is not in word, but in power. You cannot do anything without the Holy Spirit backing you, therefore seek to covet a relationship with Him. Fellowship with the Holy Spirit is where you get empowered. Until you come to the full realisation that you cannot do anything without the Holy Spirit, you will continue to strive in your strength and in vain.

The Spirit dwells in you and therefore you are His tabernacle and He will never dwell in a defiled temple. You just cannot afford to be out of tune with the Holy Spirit, for it is through the word of God and the Holy Spirit that you can ever attain any victory in the spirit realm. It is the Holy Spirit that helps us to know the things that are freely given to us of God (*1 Corinthians 2:12-13)* that we may compare spiritual things with spiritual.

I believe this is enough to convince you of the importance of the Holy Spirit in whatever God is calling you to. Remember, the calling is not always a calling to a pulpit to be a preacher. We have more records of Jesus in the streets than we do of Him behind the pulpits in the Synagogues.

The Name of Jesus

The name of Jesus is the most exalted name there is. It is the key that gives us access to eternal life. Without the name of Jesus, there is no salvation. Believing and confessing Jesus as our Lord and saviour is what gives us recognition in Heaven as children of God.

> *⁹ Wherefore God also hath highly exalted him, and given him a name which is above every name:*
> *¹⁰ That at the name of Jesus every knee should bow, of things in heaven, and things in earth, and things under the earth;*
> *¹¹ And that every tongue should confess that Jesus Christ is Lord, to the glory of God the Father.*
>
> Philippians 2:9-11

This name is what gives us recognition in Heaven. It is the signature that must be on every request you make to heaven and on every demand you make to the kingdom of darkness.

> *¹³ And I will do [I Myself will grant] whatever you ask in My Name [as presenting all that I AM], so that the Father may be glorified and extolled in (through) the Son.*
>
> John 14:13 (AMP)

In *John 16:23*, Jesus again reaffirms His commitment to make things work in our favour.

> *²³ And when that time comes, you will ask nothing of Me [you will need to ask Me no questions]. I assure you, most solemnly I tell you, that My Father will grant you whatever you ask in My Name [as presenting all that I AM].*
>
> John 16:23 (AMP)

Ephesians 1: 20-22 tells us the same thing that Jesus has been raised from the dead and is seated at the right hand of God the Father in heavenly places, far above principality, power, might and dominion, and every name that is named, not only in this world but also the one to come, and has put all things under His feet and gave Him to be head over all things to the church. There is no name here on earth or in Heaven that supersedes that of Jesus. Everything is subject to Him, it is by the name of Jesus that you can get anything from Heaven, if you scream, gravel, whisper, moan and do not make your petitions to Heaven in the name of Jesus, you efforts will be fruitless. *Colossians 2:10* clearly states that *"for in Him dwelleth all the fullness of the God head bodily, and ye are complete in Him which is the head of all principalities and power"*. All powers are subject to this name when used lawfully. As we have said, every believer has the right to use this name without doubting in your heart whether or not it will work. The name works.

The disciples of Jesus did many signs and wonders in this name. They understood that every time the name is invoked, the force of heaven responds.

> [29] *And now, Lord, behold their threatenings: and grant unto thy servants, that with all boldness they may speak thy word,*
> [30] *By stretching forth thine hand to heal; **AND THAT SIGNS AND WONDERS MAY BE DONE BY THE NAME OF THY HOLY CHILD JESUS.***
> [31] *And when they had prayed, the place was shaken where they were assembled together; and they were all filled with the Holy Ghost, and they spake the word of God with boldness.*

> Acts 4:29-31

God is no respecter of persons. What he did for the disciples, He will also do for us. Later in the books of Acts, we see God responding to the prayers of the apostles.

> [12] *And by the hands of the apostles were many signs and wonders wrought among the people; (and they were all with one accord in Solomon's porch.*

> *Acts 5:12*

Step out boldly and begin to use the name of Jesus. It will work for you if you trust Him.

The Blood of Jesus

The blood of Jesus is the sign of the covenant God has made with us. Without the blood of Jesus, there is no calling. The blood of Jesus is the price that was paid for humanity. It is the blood of justification that speaks louder than the voice of condemnation. The blood of Jesus that speaks better things than the blood of Abel.

> [24] *And to Jesus the mediator of the new covenant, and to the blood of sprinkling, that speaketh better things than that of Abel.*
> [25] *See that ye refuse not him that speaketh. For if they escaped not who refused him that spake on earth, much more shall not we escape, if we turn away from him that speaketh from heaven:*

> *Hebrews 12:24-25*

It is the blood of redemption and the seal of the new covenant. It is the blood of Jesus that makes the calling and election sure. The blood of Jesus cleanses every sin and without this blood, the power of sin is effective.

> [22] *And almost all things are by the law purged with blood; and without shedding of blood is no remission.*

> *Hebrews 9:22*

This blood makes it possible for the believer to overcome the devil. It is a force that drives back contradictions to the calling.

¹¹ And they overcame him by the blood of the Lamb, and by the word of their testimony; and they loved not their lives unto the death.

Revelation 12:11

It provides protection to the believer against all the challenges that the enemy would ever bring your way. It is a spiritual shield for you against sickness, persecution and death. This protective power of the blood was demonstrated in the old testament when the children of Israel were delivered from Egypt.

¹³ And the blood shall be to you for a token upon the houses where ye are: and when I see the blood, I will pass over you, and the plague shall not be upon you to destroy you, when I smite the land of Egypt.

Exodus 12:13

All those houses that did not have the blood on their door posts, suffered the death of their first born. They lost the symbol of strength and pride simply because they were not entitled to the covering the blood provided.

In the new testament, Christ is our Passover Lamb.

*⁷ Purge out therefore the old leaven, that ye may be a new lump, as ye are unleavened. **FOR EVEN CHRIST OUR PASSOVER IS SACRIFICED FOR US:***

1 Corinthians 5:7

1 Peter 1:19 says "...but with the precious blood of Christ, as of a lamb without blemish and without spot". Therefore the blood covers you against anything that the enemy wants to bring your way. You have the right as a believer to plead the blood of Jesus to protect you and shield you, and all that is affiliated or associated with you.

Your Understanding of Authority

Much as I would really love to say that being born again is a jolly ride of vacations, pleasantries, chill out time, pressing the snooze button of the issues that life brings and living a trouble free life, I must give you some reality check. This really is not the case. Your life as a believer is a life of battle. Why? There is an enemy against the calling you have. Whatever your calling, the god of this world is against you. This is not to scare you and put fear in you. In fact, you should be happy. The presence of this enemy gives yo the opportunity to demonstrate the God-like nature that is in you.

Though the devil is the god of this world, he does not have authority over you because you are not of this world. Where you are from, the devil has no authority. Do not mistaken the devil to be in comparison with God in spiritual hierarchy, he is an angel, a fallen angel. He fell out of grace with God his maker and was banished from heaven to earth.

> [12] *Son of man, take up a lamentation upon the king of Tyrus, and say unto him, Thus saith the Lord GOD; Thou sealest up the sum, full of wisdom, and perfect in beauty.*
> [13] *Thou hast been in Eden the garden of God; every precious stone was thy covering, the sardius, topaz, and the diamond, the beryl, the onyx, and the jasper, the sapphire, the emerald, and the carbuncle, and gold: the workmanship of thy tabrets and of thy pipes was prepared in thee in the day that thou wast created.*
> [14] *Thou art the anointed cherub that covereth; and I have set thee so: thou wast upon the holy mountain of God; thou hast walked up and down in the midst of the stones of fire.*
> [15] *Thou wast perfect in thy ways from the day that thou wast created, till iniquity was found in thee.*
>
> *Ezekiel 28:12-15*

The devil and his accomplices (*demons*) are all God's creation and are not in any way equal with God, they were all angels who rebelled against God. The authority he demonstrates here on earth is the one we have allowed him to. If he is really an authority on earth, why did he not enforce his authority when Jesus showed up in the gospels? Where was he when the disciples when out preaching and returned saying *"..even the devils were subject unto us through thy name"* (*Luke 10:17*). Did he have a chance? He was up against Jesus. Look at the description Jesus was given in the book of Colossians.

> [16] *For by him were all things created, that are in heaven, and that are in earth, visible and invisible, whether they be thrones, or dominions, or principalities, or powers: all things were created by him, and for him:*
> [17] *And he is before all things, and by him all things consist.*
>
> *Colossians 1:16-17*

I believe this lack of understanding and exercise of authority accounts for a lot of failures of believers to attain what they have aspired to. The most excellent news in it all is that you are fighting from a vantage point of victory. Jesus has already fought the hardest part of the battle and has given us victory over the enemy.

> [57] *But thanks be to God, which giveth us the victory through our Lord Jesus Christ.*
>
> *1 Corinthians 15:57*

The devil will do everything to keep you down but you must fight to stand and stand to fight. We know that there are two realms in existence, the physical realm and the spiritual realm, and things that happen in the physical realm are first birthed in the spiritual realm then incubated in the mind of a person in the physical realm. This is why you must get a good understanding of how the spirit realm works and how to deal with things in that realm. *Romans 1:20* makes us understand that invincible things are clearly seen and understood by the things made.

> ²⁰ *For the invisible things of him from the creation of the world are clearly seen, being understood by the things that are made, even his eternal power and Godhead; so that they are without excuse:*
>
> *Romans 1:20*

The things that we see are there to prove the existence of the ones we do not see.

God has made many promises available to His children and Jesus has given us authority to put the enemy under our feet. In *Luke 10:19*, Jesus empowers all believers.

> ¹⁹ *Behold, I give unto you power to tread on serpents and scorpions, and over all the power of the enemy: and nothing shall by any means hurt you.*
>
> *Luke 10:19*

This means you have all power over the devil and his cohorts, the serpent is the devil and the scorpions are his assistance the demons, they cannot hurt you unless you let them. In *Matthew 16:19*, Jesus gives the believer power beyond measure to control things in the spirit realm.

> ¹⁹ *And I will give unto thee the keys of the kingdom of heaven: and whatsoever thou shalt bind on earth shall be bound in heaven: and whatsoever thou shalt loose on earth shall be loosed in heaven.*
>
> *Matthew 16:19*

Do you realise that the binding starts on earth? The fact that Jesus referred to the kingdom of heaven which is not a physical kingdom but a spiritual one should let you know that you are dealing with things in the spirit realm. This also highlights the need for things to be bound in the spirit. If it was not important, Jesus would not have said so. This ability to bind is activated by speaking words.

Take authority over your life to ensure that the blessings, promises and inheritance God has given to you is manifested. The devil wants you bound and this bondage manifests in different ways, sickness, oppression, insanity, bareness, stagnation, failure, poverty, war, wickedness, affliction, living a meaningless life even when you work really hard, ungodly fear, blockage at the edge of miracles, generational curses, and many more such cases. All these things follow the same spiritual principle. They have their root in the spirit realm and it is only ignorance of these facts that keeps the devil in control in these areas. You are dealing with spiritual wickedness and principalities, therefore deal with the spirit behind your problem. Identify exactly what is troubling you and deal with it in prayer. Pray fervently and effectually till you see the change in your life.

> [12] *And from the days of John the Baptist until now the kingdom of heaven suffereth violence, and the violent take it by force.*
>
> *Matthew 11:12*

Press with all boldness and disarm the kingdom of darkness and posses what belongs to you, confront command, oppose, break down, bind, bring down, uproot, dismantle anything in your way because you have in you the Spirit of God, and you are complete in Jesus who is the head of all principality and power.

So really what is there to fear? You do not have any excuse whatsoever to remain in bondage because you have not received the spirit of bondage to fear again but the spirit of adoption to cry Abba Father. (*Romans 8:15*). Get up and take hold of all that belongs to you. It is time to put the enemy in his place, Jesus has done all He would ever do. He has paid the price, blotted out the hand writing of ordinances that was against you, and took it out of the way nailing it to the cross, spoiled principalities and powers and made a show of them openly triumphing over them in it.

There are battles to be fought, victories to be declared, the time of self pity, leading an unfulfilled life is so over. Take all things by the horn and take charge, enough of some silly demons tormenting you and messing with you.

Welcome to a fulfilling life. Arise and Shine for they light is come and the glory of the Lord is risen upon you. (*Isaiah 60:1*)

Can you see that God has made so much available to you to make sure you fulfil your calling in life, whatever the calling is? Being a believer is not about making you look good in addition to your clothing, it is not another fashion accessories or another title that you add to your name. Is your belief your clothing or is it a clothing accessory? You cannot be lukewarm in God's kingdom, you are either hot on fire or cold and burnt out.

What motivates you? If God does not motivate you then you are on the wrong track , if you are living your life to please other men, you inherit the wind. The very human being you try so much to please most times is not as keen or interested in pleasing you. You have a high calling of God on your life, your life should be all about Jesus, do not play church or religion, it will only lead you back where you started from, a lot of people do not quite understand what being a spiritual man or woman is. It is not about the outer ambience that people wear known as spiritual countenance, that is all pretence and religious gimmicks as the Pharisees.

A spiritual man or woman is simply one who is led by God's Spirit and is obedient to the instructions and precepts of God. Until you reach the point in your life that you thirst so much for God that it is unquenchable, you have not caught the vision yet. Do you see God as a deal that just helps you out when in need or in trouble, and you forget Him right after comfort? You need to re-evaluate yourself and your belief. What are you ready to give up for God? Have you ever asked God what you could do for Him rather than what He could do for you? Get into the programme that is far greater than you.

Your entire life time is a life of purpose and destiny, I am sure by now you know that God does not do anything without a mission or reason, you are not here on earth to add a number to the population but to do a definite thing that He has mandated you to come and fulfil here on earth. It is up to you to decide if you want to fulfil your purpose but as a believer you must seek to live a purpose driven life.

What is the value of the life you are living? How does your life affect those around you? Does your life motivate others? These are questions you should ask yourself from time to time for the rest of your life. How has my life glorified the kingdom of God and heaven? Are you just sitting around and waiting for providence to move, providence will only move when you move. Are you here to mark time, sit on the fence and watch life go by or are you here to impact the world and glorify God through your works and the gospel that you preach?

We are His workmanship, created in Christ unto good works, which God has before ordained that we should walk in them. *Jeremiah 1:5* lets us understand that before creation and inception in the womb He the Lord knew us and before we were born He had sanctified us, and ordained us prophets unto the nations. You can now see that God created you for a definite purpose, grasp that and get into the programme.

Chapter Summary

You are a complete individual in Christ Jesus and you are a friend of God.

A call is really just a stirring up for action. It is a request to adopt a thought, position or certain behavioural characteristics to bring you to a desired end.

The calling is based on a covenant which cannot be broken.

Where you are from, the devil has no authority.

If God does not motivate you then you are on the wrong track.

www.ingramcontent.com/pod-product-compliance
Lightning Source LLC
Chambersburg PA
CBHW031847090426
42741CB00005B/386